BETTER MODELS FOR DEVELOPMENT IN VIRGINIA

by Edward T. McMahon
THE CONSERVATION FUND

with Sara S. Hollberg and Shelley M.

Second Printing
September 2001

Library of Congress Control Number: 2001119012
ISBN 0-9705292-1-X

♻ *Printed on recycled paper using soy-based inks*

Contents

Acknowledgments

This document was produced by The Conservation Fund (TCF), in Arlington, Virginia. It is an adaption of an earlier publication entitled *Better Models for Development in the Shenandoah Valley,* that was produced in 1999 by The Conservation Fund in partnership with the Valley Conservation Council in Staunton, Virginia. The text was written by Edward T. McMahon, Director of Land Use Programs at The Conservation Fund with assistance from Sara Hollberg of Frazier Associates, a Staunton-based architectural and planning firm, and Shelley Mastran, a Falls Church-based planning consultant and former Director of the Rural Heritage Program at the National Trust for Historic Preservation. Photographs and other graphics were supplied by Edward McMahon, the Valley Conservation Council, and Frazier Associates, unless otherwise specified. The publication was designed by Sue Dodge and printed by Whittet Print Communications.

Advisory Committee:
Jim Brown, Realtor, Rockbridge County
Louellen Brumgard, Director, Virginia Main Street Program, Richmond
Lisa Burcham, National Trust for Historic Preservation, Washington, D.C.
Mike Chandler, Virginia Tech Community Planning Specialist, Blacksburg
John Clarke, Developer, Haymount, Caroline County
Faye Cooper, Valley Conservation Council, Staunton
Rupert Cutler, Western Virginia Land Trust, Roanoke
Lee Epstein, Director Lands Program, Chesapeake Bay Foundation, Annapolis, MD
Kim Fogle, Director of Planning, Town of Front Royal, Warren County
Catharine Gilliam, Executive Director, Community Strategies, Charlottesville
John Hall, Director, The Nature Conservancy, Virginia Coast Reserve, Nassawadox
Tom Harris, Administrator, King George County
Kat Imhoff, Executive Director, Preservation Alliance of Virginia, Charlottesville
Patricia Jackson, Executive Director, James River Association, Richmond
Marcia Joseph, Planning Consultant, Keswick
Cheryl Kilday, Director, Loudoun Tourism Council, Leesburg
David Kleppinger, Director of Economic Development, Rockbridge County
Chris Miller, President, Piedmont Environment Council, Warrenton
Bob Munson, Virginia Dept. of Conservation & Recreation, Richmond
Jeryl Phillips, Principal Planner, City of Suffolk
Trip Pollard, Senior Attorney, Southern Environmental Law Center, Charlottesville
Ed Risse, Synergy Planning Inc., Fairfax
Susan Van Wagoner, Route 50 Corridor Coalition, Middleburg
Elizabeth Waters, Former Mayor, Charlottesville
Mark Wenger, Director of Facilities, Colonial Williamsburg Foundation

The Conservation Fund gratefully acknowledges the funding assistance of the Virginia Environmental Endowment and the Prince Charitable Trust. Without their generous support, this publication would not have been possible. TCF would also like to thank the many people who contributed examples and photographs and who provided advice and input to this project.

The opinions, findings, conclusions, and recommendations in this book are those of the authors. They do not necessarily reflect the views of the funders, the members of the Advisory Committee, or The Conservation Fund.

Purpose of *Better Models*

DEVELOPMENT is a "hot" issue in Virginia. Communities across the Commonwealth are grappling with how to handle an influx of new residents and businesses. At the same time, growing traffic congestion, disappearing open space, and crowded schools are stretching local budgets and citizens' nerves. In some places the debate over how to accommodate new development is loud and acrimonious, and it is almost always cast in either/or terms—e.g., progress vs. preservation; growth vs. no growth, cities vs. suburbs.

This book was written with the belief that this kind of debate is unproductive. The truth is that development is both inevitable and desirable, but the destruction of community character and natural resources that too often accompanies growth is not. Progress does not demand degraded surroundings. Our communities can grow without destroying the beauty, history, and livability of Virginia. Instead of debating whether growth will occur, we should be discussing the patterns of development: where we put it, how we arrange it, and what it looks like. If we start from this premise, communities can more easily balance conservation with economic development.

Virginia is a Special Place

Virginia, known worldwide for its history and its beauty, has an immensely productive and pleasing natural setting, a strong economy, and neighborly communities. The state's attractiveness, business-friendly policies, and location on the

Smart growth is growth that is economically sound, environmentally friendly and supportive of community livability— growth that enhances our quality of life.

J. Ronald Terwillinger, Chairman, Urban Land Institute

mid-Atlantic coast make it certain that our population, already the 12th highest in the nation, will continue to grow.

Virginians are proud of their legacy. From Native Americans to early pioneers, from Tidewater settlers to Southside traders, from Piedmont farmers to weekend anglers, Virginia residents have long recognized the Commonwealth's natural assets: magnificent mountains, fertile farms, colorful caverns, and mighty rivers like the James, Potomac, Rappahannock, and New. Virginia is also home to some of America's most beloved national parks and historic sites: Jamestown and Yorktown, Monticello and Mount Vernon, Assateague and Appomattox, the Blue Ridge Parkway and Shenandoah National Park, to name a few. And Virginia shares the Chesapeake Bay, one of the most diverse and productive estuaries in the world.

We should respect the land. It is our birthright, and almost every inch of it is densely layered with our history. For all sorts of economic, social, and psychological reasons, we should do more to protect the land, and we should recognize that the landscape is the setting for all our architecture. New buildings can either intrude on the landscape, or they can be designed and sited so that they fit in. This book provides some ideas on how to fit buildings with the landscape.

We're Losing Ground

Every day in America people make decisions about where to live, where to invest, or where to vacation based on communities' scenic, natural, and historic assets. When people visit Virginia, what do they expect to find? Healthy downtowns, unspoiled countryside, uncrowded highways, beautiful beaches, uncommon communities, a bountiful Bay, and a unique sense of place. This is the image of our state—a reflection of its special character.

But is this really what we still see? Over the past 40 years, Virginia has grown so rapidly that, unfortunately, much of the new development is ill-planned and unattractive. Between 1960 and 1990, Virginia's metropolitan areas expanded three times faster than population growth. Since 1982, Virginia has lost more than 920,800 acres of farmland and forest to development. Traffic congestion is increasing, and haphazard new development is rapidly eroding the very character that makes Virginia unique.

Northern Virginia, for example, is one of the fastest-growing areas in America. Its subdivisions, shopping centers, office parks, and ever widening roads are spreading from county to county. Despite spending billions on new schools and transportation projects, roads are congested, schools are overcrowded, local governments are fiscally strained, natural resources are threatened, and communities are losing their sense of place. Sprawling development threatens the entire I-95

Smart growth is pro-growth. We know that developers, banks and the entire community rely on growth to fuel the economy. The goal is not to limit growth but to channel it to areas where infrastructure allows growth to be sustained over the long term.

Hugh McCall, Jr.,
Chairman, Bank of America

corridor between Washington and Richmond, the I-64 corridor between Charlottesville and Chesapeake, and much of the I-81 corridor through the Shenandoah Valley.

In the Piedmont, when a farmer dies, often the next thing to crop out of the ground is a sign advertising "lots for sale." In southwest Virginia, beautiful views of the mountains are increasingly marred by giant signs touting fast food and gasoline. On the Eastern Shore and Northern Neck, riverfronts and marshes are threatened with a proliferation of second-home and resort developments. Even in economically distressed areas like Southside Virginia, the little growth that does occur often takes place on the strip outside of town. Add to that, look-alike chain stores, big-box retailers, gaudy service stations, and soulless subdivisions. Too often, the results are so brash, monotonous, or out of place that many citizens cringe at the prospect of more new development.

It is no wonder that national organizations have recognized parts of Virginia as "endangered." In 1995 the National Trust for Historic Preservation named the Northern Piedmont one of America's 11 Most Endangered Historic Places, and in 1998 the Chancellorsville Battlefield was added to the list. Likewise, in 1997 the American Farmland Trust named the Northern Piedmont one of America's 20 Most Threatened Agricultural Areas. And in 1999 Scenic America listed the area between Route 15 and I-81 north of Warrenton and New Market as one of America's "Last Chance Landscapes."

Shenandoah Valley farm

Downtown, Lexington

This book showcases such projects. These real-life examples, in contrast to the image of standard development, are glimpses into one possible future—a future that accommodates growth without sacrificing our communities. The coming decades will determine what subsequent generations will experience here. Either we replicate the unsatisfying building patterns of other parts of the country, or we choose a better way to grow.

Most Virginians love the land and support measures to protect it. Public opinion surveys and local planning and visioning exercises demonstrate this. A 1999 poll by Virginia Commonwealth University found that a majority of Virginians favor better growth management and are concerned about traffic congestion and sprawl. Likewise, a 1997 poll found that the top reason Virginians enjoy living in the Commonwealth is "having access to places of natural beauty, such as mountains or rivers." Similarly, a 1996 Virginia Outdoors Survey found that 87% of respondents said that protecting open space and other visual resources was " important" or "very important." Virginians want better development, but they haven't always taken the necessary steps to achieve it.

Millions of personal choices seem harmless enough when taken one at a time, but they add up to the suburban sprawl that has devastated Virginia ecosystems.

James A. Bacon,
"Tyranny of Small Decisions,"
Virginia Business

Better Models should not be seen as a call for more regulation. Rather, it is a call for a more thoughtful approach to new development. Successful communities use education, incentives, and voluntary initiatives—not just regulation. Many of the projects featured here were undertaken by individuals of their own accord. At the same time, it is clear that local governments could use additional planning tools and resources to better manage growth. In the meantime, creative use of existing tools, including strong zoning, corridor overlays, design guidelines, the proffer system, and conservation easements, can help result in better development.

Using *Better Models*

This publication presents six principles for better development. These principles are meant to protect the countryside, strengthen existing communities and improve the suburbs. Each principle is illustrated with numerous examples of alternatives to conventional development. There are many such models throughout Virginia and across the nation. Downtowns are being rejuvenated, open space is being preserved, historic buildings are being restored, and walkable, mixed-use developments are being constructed.

Sustainable Technology Park, Northampton County

Six Principles for Better Development

1. Conserve Virginia's Natural and Scenic Assets

The first principle of better development is identifying where not to develop. Successful communities always identify the areas that are most important to preserve, whether it is farmland, forests, riparian corridors, natural areas, scenic views, or wildlife habitat. Every community needs an open space protection plan and the resources to implement it. Communities that have a blueprint for conservation are more amenable to accommodating growth in the areas where it is most appropriate. On the other hand, when citizens think all land is up for grabs, they often oppose development everywhere. Conserving natural and scenic assets is also important because farmland, forests, and scenic landscapes contribute to the economic vitality of our communities.

2. Maintain a Clear Edge between Town and Countryside

Virginia has many strong cities and towns as well as healthy rural landscapes. Safeguarding the rural character of Virginia means maintaining a clear edge between cities, towns, and countryside. This can be done by protecting open space while encouraging more compact, walkable communities. It also means encouraging infill development on vacant, underused or overlooked land, including brownfields. By maintaining this clear edge, Virginia can preserve its rural landscapes and at the same time enhance the vitality of its existing communities.

3. Build Livable Communities

Attractive and livable communities are the flip side of protecting rural character. Livable communities have a balance of jobs, homes, services, and amenities. Livable communities are walkable and pedestrian-friendly. They're also well designed and attractive. Healthy downtowns are especially important because they are the heart and soul of Virginia communities and the distinctive image that people take with them. We can even reshape the strip to make it more appealing and functional. Wherever new development occurs, location, scale, siting, and design decisions should be carefully considered.

4. Preserve Historic Resources

Virginia's rich history is still evident in the wealth of historic and archaeological sites found in cities, small towns and rural areas throughout the state. Historic assets should be identified and protected, and developers should be encouraged to rehabilitate and reuse historic structures. Protecting historic resources such as Civil War battlefields or small-town main streets is also important because historic preservation is a powerful tool for economic revitalization that generates jobs and attracts tourists and investors.

5. Respect Local Character in New Construction

Eighty percent of everything ever built in America has been built since the end of World War II, and much of it is cookie-cutter, off-the-shelf junk. New buildings can either complement the character of Virginia communities or they can turn our state into "Anyplace USA." Virginia communities should do more to ensure that new construction—particularly chain stores, shopping centers, and franchises—respect local character. Virginia's natural setting, historical development pattern, and architectural traditions make this a distinctive place. By identifying what makes each community unique, and what harms that uniqueness, localities can develop standards that encourage new construction to complement existing community character.

6. Reduce the Impact of the Car

Reducing the impact of the automobile means providing more transportation choice. It also means designing transportation facilities that are beautiful as well as functional, that meet the needs of people as well as those of motor vehicles, and that respect local communities. Standards for neighborhood streets, roads and bridges should be reexamined to make them more human-scale and community friendly. Even minor design improvements can lessen the negative visual and environmental impacts of new roads and bridges. Transportation choice can be expanded by providing better public transportation and building more sidewalks and bike paths. Communities can also foster healthy neighborhoods by considering traffic-calming measures to slow down traffic.

Economics and Environment Can Work Together

DEVELOPMENT does not have to mean destruction of the things that people love. The models presented in this book prove that economic development and environmental protection can be compatible. In fact, maintaining the natural and historical integrity of our state is fundamentally important to our economic well-being. Livable communities have more choices. To sell short our natural and cultural assets will cost us more in the long run—socially, economically, and environmentally. Increasingly, communities across the country are recognizing this link.

It's Our Choice

Virginia communities have a choice about how they grow, and these choices have consequences that can last a lifetime. But too often the debate over development is seen as an either/or contest: development or no development, progress or preservation. A more useful framing of the issues is to concentrate on "how" and "where" we develop. Once we define what is damaging or unsatisfying about conventional development, we can address those concerns. The three critical elements are the location, the arrangement, and the design of new development.

We can grow without eroding the special character of our communities. We can grow and still have a strong economy, lots of open space, walkable neighborhoods, good schools, and a healthy environment. It's a matter of choice. Each community can choose how it develops, but if we accept the lowest common denominator in new development, that is what we will get. When we set higher standards, we can achieve higher results. All of us, citizens, elected officials, builders, environmentalists, and community leaders, can determine the future of our Virginia communities—if we put a high enough priority on identifying the things we really care about.

Conservation is a state of harmony between man and the land.

Aldo Leopold

Sometimes builders argue that if people didn't like what they produced, consumers wouldn't buy it. This is a vastly oversimplified version of what's really going on. Many homebuyers buy homes in communities that they know are flawed. They buy because of location, the quality of local schools, or the price—even though they might prefer very different neighborhoods and commercial areas if they were offered. This book is based on the belief that there are better, more attractive, and more profitable ways to build.

Building a Shared Vision

No place will retain its special character by accident. Successful communities always have a "vision" for the future. And often the communities that have a design-oriented vision are among the most desirable and economically sound in the nation. Working to maintain a distinctive local identity can pay off.

The key is for each community to develop its own shared vision for the future and raise expectations throughout the state. This sense of shared future throughout Virginia is especially critical for regional issues like transportation, landscape protection and heritage tourism. Only with widespread recognition of what makes our state special do we have a chance to safeguard the treasure that is VIRGINIA.

Necessary Elements for Success

Preservation of Virginia's unique character relies on a few key actions:

- Committing statewide to the goal of preserving Virginia's special character
- Identifying and preserving important natural, scenic, and historic assets
- Building local economic development and land use plans around the preservation and enhancement of key assets

- Raising the level of expectation for the quality of new development
- Meeting the needs of both landowners and the community
- Paying attention to aesthetics as well as economics and ecology
- Assessing the impacts of land use policies
- Using incentives, education, and voluntary initiatives, not just regulations
- Recognizing the link between land use and transportation planning

Who Can Help
- Individual citizens
- Builders and developers
- Local business and citizen groups
- Local governments
- Nonprofit conservation and preservation organizations
- State agencies

The protection of Virginia's sense of place depends on all of us. With a widespread ethic that this issue is important, our state can remain not just a special place that reflects what was given to us, but a special place where new development adds to this legacy.

FOR MORE INFORMATION:

Balancing Nature and Commerce in Gateway Communities, Island Press, 1997; (800) 828-1302.

Land Use in America, by Henry L. Diamond and Patrick F. Noonan, Island Press, 1996; (800) 828-1302.

The Practice of Sustainable Development, by Douglas Porter, Urban Land Institute, 2000; (800) 321-5011.

Barriers to Better Development

BETTER DEVELOPMENT can be more profitable, more attractive, and more convenient than conventional sprawl-type development. It makes more efficient use of land, provides more transportation choice, reduces costs for new infrastructure, and is more respectful of Virginia's beauty and history. However, despite these benefits, smart growth represents only a small portion of recent development in Virginia. This is because applying the better development principles is often more difficult and costly than conventional development for several reasons. The key impediments to better development are:

Inflexible Local Regulations

Local regulations are often an impediment to smart growth. Most local zoning and subdivision regulations make it easier and faster to build conventional, single-use suburban-type development. Local officials should make zoning and subdivision regulations more flexible so as to encourage cluster development, mixed uses, narrower streets, and other better development concepts.

Outdated Market Perceptions

Smart development is an unfamiliar market to many developers and, as such, it is perceived as risky. Outdated assumptions often inform current market and demographic analysis. This prevents developers from building projects for significant groups of consumers with specific needs, tastes, and preferences. For example, empty nesters, retirees, unrelated singles and younger couples are all growing market segments that crave more walkable, urbane neighborhoods. Yet the market provides them with few choices.

High Development and Process Costs

Local fees and costs for development which fail to factor in the benefits of smart development, increased land and construction costs, and a shortage of suitable infill sites make smart growth more expensive and complicated. Local and state governments need to pro-

vide incentives for the reuse of historic structures, brownfield development, downtown revitalization, and other infill projects.

Financing by Formula

A lack of comparables, the secondary financing market, and bank structures and procedures can make securing financing for better development projects difficult. In general, bankers fund projects in a formulaic way, so that only standard types of developments, with predictable outcomes, receive investment. In addition, excessive parking requirements that are often imposed by lenders add expense and may conflict with the goals of both the developer and the community.

Lack of Community Involvement

Many worthy projects including both greenfield development and urban infill projects have met with community opposition. A lack of public education often translates into community opposition, even when the community supports the overall goal of smart development. A greater emphasis on high quality, place-responsive design could also greatly alleviate opposition to new development.

Public Infrastructure Subsidies

The willingness of state and local government to pay for new roads, utilities, and schools which service far-flung greenfield development encourages sprawl while increasing the cost of government services. Smart capital investments can encourage revitalization of existing communities and facilitate new development on vacant or underutilized land already served by roads and other public services.

Low Expectations

All development is not created equal. Communities that set higher standards get higher results, but some local officials are afraid to say "no" to poor quality development. Successful communities know that if they reject poor quality development, they will almost always get better development in its place. This is because most businesses will readily meet higher standards to be in an economically profitable location.

Adapted from *Principles of Smart Development,* American Planning Association, 1998.

FOR MORE INFORMATION:

Guiding Growth in Virginia: Local Incentives for Revitalization and Preservation, Environmental Law Institute, 1616 P Street, N.W., Washington, DC 20036, 1998; (800) 433-5120.

Principles of Smart Development, PAS Report #479, American Planning Association, 1998; (312) 786-6344.

Smart Growth: Myth and Fact, by the Urban Land Institute, 1999; (800) 321-5011.

Identifying Your Assets

LOCATION…location…location. Successful communities know where their assets lie. If a community's character, as expressed through its natural, scenic, and historic assets, is to be safeguarded, the first step is identifying the location and significance of particularly important features. Among these might be historic buildings, sites and neighborhoods, or natural resources such as riparian areas, special habitats, prime agricultural soils, large blocks of contiguous forest land, steep slopes, and scenic views.

Recognizing what is important is the first step toward better development. Once citizens clarify what they care about, it is easier to find strategies to protect special places or irreplaceable resources. A clear consensus on conservation can also give direction to elected officials and offer builders and developers more certainty and predictability about development.

The key to protecting the natural environment is first to protect critical environmental areas such as rivers, streams, wetlands, and steep slopes, then to protect the working landscapes: the farms and forests that automatically enhance scenic views and protect natural habitat. Keeping large tracts in productive use is also essential to assure the critical mass needed to support a resource-based economy. The "rural heritage" of Virginia has meaning and relevance for all state residents, whether you live in a city, suburb, or rural area.

Enhancing the built environment relies first on protecting historic places—buildings, neighborhoods, and landscapes—and second, on ensuring that new construction respects community character. New buildings, whether stores, homes, offices, or government buildings, should be good neighbors and respect the landscape. The historic fabric of Virginia's towns and cities is one of the most important characteristics of our state, and it is vital to the health of our tourism industry .

Tools to Use:

Resource Inventories - Specific resources, including natural areas, historic sites, open space, scenic views, prime farmland, and so on, can be identified, described, and mapped. The process of inventorying key resources can be undertaken by citizen groups, private organizations, or public agencies—or a coalition of such groups. These inventories can be indispensable for building community awareness and consensus and for planning the future.

Visual Assessments - Numerous visual assessment techniques are available for citizens to use in understanding and evaluating their communities. These include using geographic information systems (GIS) to map special places in the community, designing a tour, taking photographs of typical scenes in the community, or studying aerial photographs. All enhance citizens' awareness of how their community is laid out and how it looks—with an eye toward planning how it might look in the future.

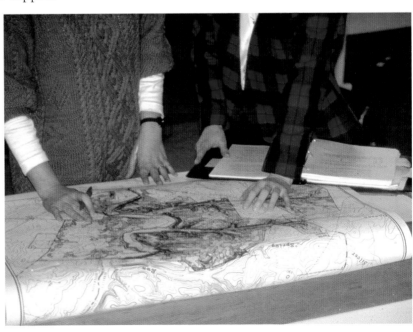

Visual Preference Surveys - Citizens view slides of various types of local development and give them either negative or positive ratings. Discussion of the results clarifies what makes a development project pleasing or disappointing and helps pinpoint what citizens care most about. Visual preference surveys can be conducted simply by having people photograph what they most like and what they least like in their community, and then comparing the results in a community forum.

Visual Simulations - Alternative designs of a shopping center, a road corridor, or a subdivision can be simulated by various means so that citizens can see what future development will look like. Such simulations can be accomplished through drawings, models, or computer graphics. The most realistic simulations are usually achieved through computers and video technology.

Community Visioning - Citizens and local leaders are led through a series of exercises that help them identify community assets as well as community weaknesses or opportunities, in order to articulate what they think the community should be like in the future. This "vision" can then be established as a goal for policy making, and various strategies can be developed to achieve that goal.

Design Charrettes - Through a community workshop, citizens assisted by professional landscape architects, architects, or planners, can work to develop solutions to community design problems. For example, a charrette might focus on streetscape design, gateways, a community park, or protection of views from a road.

FOR MORE INFORMATION:

A Guide to Community Visioning, 3rd Edition, by Steven Ames, American Planning Association, 1998; (312) 786-6344.

Geographic Information Systems, 2nd Edition, by David Martin, American Planning Association, 1996; (312) 786-6344,

O, Say Can You See: A Visual Awareness Tool Kit for Communities, Scenic America, 1999; (202) 543-6200.

Choices for Virginia Communities

Farmland Preservation

Riparian Buffers

Street Trees

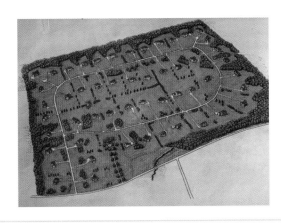
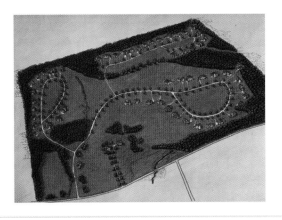

Open Space Development

Choices for Virginia Communities

**Tree
Preservation**

**Rural
Development**

Downtowns

**Suburban
Housing**

Choices for Virginia Communities

Community Gateways

Parking Lot Landscaping

Historic Sites

Shopping Centers

Choices for Virginia Communities

**Walkable
Neighborhoods**

**New
Subdivisions**

Townhouses

**Residential
Street
Standards**

Protect Farm and Forest Land

Would you rather see cows or concrete on Virginia farmland?

Agriculture is one of Virginia's most important industries. Likewise, the forest products industry contributes substantially to the wealth of our state, yet these industries face many challenges. One of the greatest of these is encroaching suburbanization.

Farmland is critical to Virginia's economic health not just because of the value of the products it generates, but also because it contributes to the state's economy as scenic assets. Virginia's working landscapes of farms and forests attract new businesses and wealth to our communities, increase property values throughout the state, and support our tourism economy. Farmland and forests also play a key role in sustaining healthy natural systems by providing plant and wildlife habitat and

Farmland lost

migration corridors, watershed protection, and other benefits.

Today, vast areas of the state remain in forest, a renewable resource that pumps the rural economy while providing aesthetic, recreational, and environmental benefits.

Despite the vital contribution that farmland and forests make to our local economies, farmers and forest landowners currently receive little financial return from communities for their contribution to local quality of life. Even the most profitable farms are often less lucrative than selling land for subdivisions.

Looking to the future, if agriculture is to remain a vital element of Virginia's economy, state, regional, and local leaders will have to ensure the long-term economic viability and productivity of our state's agricultural lands. We can identify and aggressively pursue ways to make it possible and desirable for private landowners to keep their land part of the working landscape.

THINGS YOU SHOULD KNOW:

■ In 1997 agriculture accounted for more than $19.5 billion in economic activity in Virginia.

■ Nearly 1 in 7 Virginia workers is dependent on agriculture or related industries.

■ Virginia lost more than 467,000 acres of farmland and forests between 1992 and 1997, double the rate of land conversion between 1982 and 1992.

■ In 1997 Virginia's northern Piedmont was ranked the second most threatened farmland region in the U.S. by the American Farmland Trust.

■ The Hampton Roads area lost one-third of its farmland between 1959 to 1992. Nearby James City County lost 69% of its farms and York County lost 84% of its farmland since 1959.

■ Numerous studies across the nation show that farms generate taxes but require few public services. For example, an Augusta County study found that farm and forest landowners, even at land-use tax rates, paid $1.24 million more in taxes than they received in services in fiscal year 1996; in contrast, residential uses ran a $8.73 million deficit.

■ In Fauquier County, a unit of farmland, forest, or open space costs only 15 cents in services for every tax dollar it generates (a ratio of 1 to .15). In Rappahannock County, this ratio is 1 to .17; in Culpeper County, 1 to .19. In James City County, an average residential unit costs $2.56 in services for every $1.00 of tax revenue it generates.

■ In Loudoun County, horse farms generate on average $89 million per year in sales, $78 million in operating expenses and provide employment for 2,480 people.

■ Timber is the #2 crop in the state, behind poultry and eggs, and the forest products industry accounts for one in six manufacturing jobs.

■ Altogether, the harvesting, processing, and marketing of timber products adds $9.8 billion to Virginia's economy. Another $1.7 billion is generated by forest-related wildlife and recreation.

■ For every $1.00 received by a timber landowner, an estimated $48.64 in total value is added to Virginia's economy.

■ Between 1992 and 1997, Virginia lost an average of 93,440 acres of forest and farmland annually, mostly due to development. Most of the loss is in the coastal plain and the northern Piedmont.

Form Agricultural and Forestal Districts

In past years the rural nature of much of Virginia was so self-evident as to not require special agricultural zones. However, today scattered residential and commercial development is making it increasingly important for farmers to form agricultural and forestal districts. Farmers in many areas of the state already have taken this option.

Agricultural and forestal districts are voluntary conservation measures. They are a contract between the local government and property owners spelling out that no new, non-agricultural uses will take place in the district for a specified time.

Property owners in agricultural or forestal districts commit to keeping their land in farming or forestry for a term of between four and ten years. In return, the locality must recognize the district in its local planning and zoning. While ag districts are only a temporary fix, district status does have an impact. An ag district is a powerful image on a land use map, declaring that an area is reserved for farming and is off limits for suburban-style development. The process of organizing the district, and the certainty of continuity, can strengthen the farming community. There are also financial benefits for the landowners.

THINGS YOU SHOULD KNOW:

■ Agricultural and forestal districts are used in at least 29 Virginia counties and cover more than 725,000 acres of farmland.

■ Agricultural districts range widely in size, with a minimum of 200 contiguous acres. There is no min-

imum acreage for each landowner and no maximum on the size of the district. A single property owner can create a district.

■ Cities can have agricultural districts too.

■ Landowners in agricultural districts receive land-use tax rates, which means landowners may pay lower property taxes.

Landowner Benefits of Agricultural and Forestal Districts:
• Guaranteed land-use tax rates
• Protection from nuisance ordinances for customary farming or forestry practices
• Locality must consider the ag district in local land-use decisions, such as rezonings
• State agencies must consider the impact of their actions on farming and forestry in ag districts
• Greater protection from land condemnation

Tools to Protect Farmland and Open Space

Protecting farmland, forests, and open space requires not only protecting a productive and sufficient land base but also addressing the many financial and legal stresses on the rural way of life.

Without resource-based industries, there is little chance of retaining the rural landscape that distinguishes large parts of Virginia. The key to long-term farmland and forest preservation is to reduce development pressure, while appropriately protecting property rights. An effective strategy must be two-pronged. It must limit the potential for non-agricultural uses in rural areas. At the same time, it must provide the stability and financial resources to help farmers stay in business. Farmers need a critical mass of farmland, but they also need to maintain the value of their primary asset—their land.

Agricultural district in Rockingham County

Much of the character and beauty of the countryside also derives from nonagricultural open space. Such land may be valuable as wetland, wildlife habitat, historic landscape, scenic vista, park land, or biological preserve. The key to protecting this land is to ensure that its value is recognized—both in planning documents and by the public at large—so that it will not be developed or destroyed.

Planning Tools You Can Use:

Land Conservation Funds - Most East Coast states, including North Carolina, Maryland, Pennsylvania, Delaware, and New Jersey, have created dedicated funds for land conservation. Although Virginia has lagged behind other states in funding land conservation, in 1999 the Commonwealth established the Virginia Land Conservation Foundation, and in 2000 the General Assembly appropriated $12.4 million for land and easement acquisition for a two-year period. The money will be used to preserve and protect valuable open spaces, natural areas, and historic sites—including battlefields.

Purchase of Development Rights - Purchase of development rights (PDR) programs pay landowners for restricting the future use of their land. After selling an easement, the landowner retains all other rights of ownership, including the right to farm the land. The City of Virginia Beach has used the PDR concept to pay for easements over prime farm and forest land in

its Agricultural Reserve. Since 1995, the city has purchased the development rights on almost 4,000 acres and directly preserved approximately 350 sites from non-agricultural development. This voluntary program costs the city less than half the capital expenses that would be required if the land were built out at current zoning. Contact: Director of Agriculture, Virginia Beach Department of Agriculture, (757) 426-5775.

Transfer of Development Rights (TDR) - TDR programs allow landowners to transfer the right to develop a parcel of land to another parcel of land. In the context of farmland preservation, TDRs are used to shift development from agricultural areas to designated growth zones closer to urban services. TDR is a technique used primarily by counties and municipalities but it involves the private marketplace. TDR programs differ from the purchase of development rights in that transactions are between private landowners and developers. Local governments in Maryland, New Jersey, New York, and other states have used TDR programs. Montgomery County, Maryland, for example, has protected more than 47,000 acres in its agricultural reserve through its TDR program. Unfortunately, at this time there is no enabling legislation in Virginia that allows Commonwealth communities to use TDRs.

Exclusive Agricultural Zones - Agricultural zones designate areas where farming is the primary land use and nonagricultural land uses are discouraged. The best-known and most successful program in agricultural zoning is in Oregon, which has a statewide demarcation of exclusive agricultural areas in which uses incompatible with farming are not permitted. Here in Virginia, Isle of Wight County has designated 70 percent of the county as a Rural/Agricultural Conservation District. Some low-density residential development is allowed, with densities based on a sliding scale or on achieving desired development standards. Generally, the more open space preserved and the more compact the development design, the higher the density allowed. Contact: Isle of Wight County Director of Planning and Zoning, (757) 357-3191.

Dedicated Funding Source - Throughout America communities use a variety of dedicated funding sources to pay for land conservation or parkland acquisition. Some of these include sales taxes, real-estate transfer taxes, lottery proceeds, license plate sales, parking garage revenues, and general obligation bonds. For example, in 1998 Fairfax County approved an $87 million park bond. Each year, James City County sets aside a portion of its real estate tax rate for purchasing open space, including farmland. This funding has allowed the county to acquire a large farm near Jamestown and other key properties. Contact: James City County, (757) 253-6671.

Special Districts - To provide a steady stream of funds for parks and open space, hundreds of communities have created special districts. Special districts can serve a city, a county, a portion of a county, or a combination of cities and counties. Special park districts can finance their services and facilities directly without having to compete with other infrastructure needs. In 1959, the Northern Virginia Regional Park Authority (NVRPA) was created to serve Arlington, Fairfax, and Loudoun counties along with the cities of Alexandria, Falls Church, and Fairfax. Operating funds come from park rentals, fees, and services. Acquisition funds come from semi-annual park bonds and other county and city funds. Contact NVRPA, (703) 352-5950.

Mandatory Open Space Requirements - Mandatory open space requirements are specified percentages of land parcels that must be kept undeveloped. Fauquier County requires that 85% of tracts in rural areas be retained in permanent open space when development occurs. Contact: Fauquier County Chief of Planning, (540) 347-8703.

Sliding Scale Zoning - Sliding scale zoning attempts to concentrate development by placing different restrictions on land depending on the size of the parcel. As the size of the parcel increases, the number of dwelling units allowed in relation to the total area decreases. This protects the right to add dwelling units to smaller parcels while forestalling large-scale, dense development on rural tracts. Clarke County was the first locality in the state to use sliding scale zoning. Clarke County also sets a maximum lot size for dwellings placed on prime farmland. Contact: Clarke County Planning Director, (540) 955-5132.

Large-Lot Zoning - Some communities adopt large-lot zoning in the hope of slowing development and preserving open space. Large-lot zoning establishes a

Four Development Options for the Fringe Countryside on 50-Acre Sites

1. **Suburban pod** 50 units on one-acre lots

2. **Large residential lots** 10 five-acre lots

3. **Cluster development of 25 units and 25 acres of open space**

4. **Agricultural zoning at one dwelling per 50 acres**

DIAGRAM BY TOM DANIELS

low ratio of dwelling units to parcel size (e.g., one house per 10 acres, 20 acres, or 50 acres). Unfortunately, the typical large-lot zone in Virginia is two to ten acres. This does little to preserve the countryside. It scatters residential development, separates neighbors, and makes school busing expensive. Residential lots of two to ten acres eat up the landscape in large chunks, creating parcels "too big to mow and too small to farm." It also is difficult to have a sense of community in a large-lot subdivision. For example, try borrowing a cup of sugar or going trick-or-treating on Halloween in a large-lot subdivision. However, large-lot subdivisions can reduce the cost of public services and save open space if the lots are big enough to protect rural uses. In the Napa and Sonoma Valleys of California, large-lot zoning is one house per 100 acres or more. In Maryland, large-lot zoning is one house per 25 to 50 acres. In Virginia, Rappahannock County has a 25-acre zone, and Essex, Albemarle, and several other counties have 20-acre zoning in certain areas. Contacts: Albemarle County Planning Department, (804) 296-5823; Rappahannock County Zoning Department, (540) 675-3342.

You don't know what you got til it's gone.

Joni Mitchell

Statewide Efforts- Many states have policies and programs designed to protect farmland and open space that can serve as models for Virginia. For example, Pennsylvania spends more than $40 million each year purchasing the development rights on farmland. Likewise, the state of Maryland's extensive open space protection programs have permanently protected approximately 360,000 acres of farmland and open space. The tools used in Maryland include the following:

- *Easements-* The Maryland Agricultural Land Preservation Program (MALPP), funded by real–estate transfer taxes and by taxes assessed on agricultural land converted to non-agricultural uses, funds the purchase of permanent easements on farmland. Priority is given to easements with the lowest value. MALPP protected almost 167,000 acres of farmland in its first 14 years.

- *County Farmland Protection Programs -* State certification (and the retention of 75% of the agricultural transfer tax revenues generated in that county) is offered to any county that demonstrates it has an effective program to preserve farmland. By 1999, 15 of Maryland's 23 counties had been certified. In addition to purchasing easements, the counties use a variety of other techniques to protect farmland, including transfer of development rights and agricultural protection zoning. For example, Montgomery County has preserved 47,000 acres of farmland by using a Transfer of Development Rights program, and Baltimore County zones its agricultural districts at one house per 50 acres.

- *Rural Legacy Program -* Under the Maryland Rural Legacy Program approved in 1997, the state works with local governments and land trusts to purchase conservation easements on open spaces that also have important natural, cultural, or agricultural resource values. Bonds will support the program at the level of $71 to $90 million during the first five years, with perhaps between $243 - $455 million over 15 years. Contact: Program Open Space, (410) 260-8403.

FOR MORE INFORMATION:

The Economic Benefits of Parks and Open Space, by Steve Lerner and William Poole, Trust for Public Land, 1999; (800) 714-LAND.

Saving American Farmland: What Works, by the American Farmland Trust, Washington, D.C.; (202) 659-5170.

Saving America's Countryside, 2nd Edition, by Samuel N. Stokes, A. Elizabeth Watson and Shelley S. Mastran, The Johns Hopkins University Press, Baltimore, MD, 1997; (800) 537-5487.

Use Conservation Easements

As a landowner, what legacy would you like to leave? You can develop your land, or you can choose to permanently shield it from development. The land on the right has a conservation easement and will never be developed.

CONSERVATION EASEMENTS, widely used in the upper Piedmont region of the state, are becoming increasingly popular throughout Virginia. For a variety of reasons, many Virginia landowners have chosen this legal tool to protect farmland, forests, riparian zones, natural areas and historic sites. One solution to reducing the pressure on Virginia's open space is to increase the use of conservation easements to protect farmland, forests and other resources. Conservation easements protect millions of acres of land throughout the United States. The Virginia Outdoors Foundation, the state-chartered and funded land trust that is responsible for holding most of the conservation easements in the Commonwealth, currently holds easements on nearly 136,000 acres.

What Is a Conservation Easement?

A conservation easement is a legal agreement between a landowner and a land trust that permanently limits uses of land in order to protect its conservation values. It allows the landowner to continue to own and use the land, to sell it or pass it on to heirs. Most conservation easements restrict uses that

With an easement you don't give up anything you would reasonably want to do, but this is one thing that you can do that will still make a difference 100 years from now.

Augusta County
Easement Donor

harm natural, scenic or historic resources while continuing to allow traditional uses such as farming and forestry.

What Is a Land Trust?

Land trusts are local, regional or statewide organizations that are involved in protecting important land resources for public benefit. The land trust or easement holder is responsible for seeing that the wishes of the landowner are upheld by future owners of the land.

How Do Easements Work?

Placing an easement on land does not mean that it cannot be developed at all. The owner states the types of development he wants to prohibit. For example, an easement on a farm might allow continued farming and the building of additional agricultural structures or it might apply to just a portion of the property. A property subject to an easement can still be sold, rented, bequeathed or otherwise transferred but the conservation easement is recorded with the deed and passed on to future holders of the land.

Conservation easements protect seaside farms on Virginia's Eastern Shore

Conservation easement protecting mountain habitat, Highland County

What Are the Benefits of Conservation Easements?

■ **Permanent Protection -** Easements ensure current owners that their property remains largely undeveloped in perpetuity. There are few things one can control after death. With an easement, landowners can protect the things they value most about their property, both now and in the future.

■ **Continued Private Ownership -** Land protected by a conservation easement is still private property. Most easements do not change the way private land is used. Land under easement can continue to play a role in the local economy through agriculture, forestry

or other activities. An easement does not require public access to the property, and the land is protected from trespass just as any other private property.

■ **Each Easement Is Unique -** Conservation easements meet the specific requirements of landowners and fit the property they protect. An easement for a small property, such as a family camp, might be quite different from one designed for a large working farm. Some owners prohibit all new construction or subdivisions, while others reserve the right to subdivide and sell some parcels for financial reasons or for one or more new home sites for their children.

■ **Lower Taxes -** Conservation easements provide financial benefits to landowners who protect their land. Easements reduce federal and state income taxes, estate taxes and capital gains taxes. The federal tax code considers the donation of a permanent conservation easement to be a charitable contribution, the value of which is tax deductible. In addition, property under conservation easements must be given land use rates for real property taxes.

THINGS YOU SHOULD KNOW:

■ More than 5.2 million acres of land are protected nationwide by local and regional land trusts. Conservation easements protect more than 140,000 acres in Virginia.

■ In 1966, the General Assembly created the Virginia Outdoors Foundation (VOF) to promote the preservation of open space in the Commonwealth. VOF accomplishes its mission primarily through the acceptance of donated conservation easements.

■ In addition to VOF, there are more than a dozen local and regional land trusts in Virginia. These include the Piedmont Environmental Council, the Valley Conserva-

Conservation easements are a way to save your view and get a tax break too.

Jean Hocker,
Land Trust Alliance

tion Council and the Western Virginia Land Trust. For more information on Virginia land trusts, see the appendix.

- In 1997, Virginia established the Open Space Preservation Trust Fund to help landowners with the legal and appraisal costs of donated conservation easements. The fund can also be used to purchase easements.

- On Virginia's Eastern Shore, the Nature Conservancy has used conservation easements to protect waterfront farms and coastal marshes from high density residential and resort development.

- Conservation easements protect the viewshed of George Washington's home at Mount Vernon.

- Tuckahoe Plantation in Goochland County and many other historic properties are protected by easements.

FOR MORE INFORMATION:

Conservation Easement Handbook, by Janet Diehl and Thomas Barrett, Land Trust Alliance, 1988; (202) 638-4725.

Protecting the Land: Conservation Easements, Past, Present and Future, by Julie Ann Gustanski and Roderick Squires, Island Press, 2000; (800) 828-1302.

Land Trust Alliance, 1331 H Street, N.W., Suite 400, Washington, DC 20005-4711; (202) 638-4725.

Virginia Outdoors Foundation, 203 Governor Street, Richmond, VA 23219; (804) 225-2147.

Your local land trust (see Appendix).

Preserve Scenic Views and Vistas

Would you prefer to see views that look like this?

Or views that look like this?

SUCCESSFUL COMMUNITIES always strive for development that is not only fiscally and environmentally sound, but visually pleasing as well. Protecting scenic views and vistas is an increasingly important goal and not just for aesthetic reasons. From coast to coast, communities see visual resources as an integral part of their economic well being. In fact, you can put a dollar value on a view. Scenic landscapes are an asset not just because you or I think they are nice but because other people are willing to pay to see the view and to experience the unique character of a place.

Visually attractive areas can be found throughout Virginia. Some are national, even international in renown. Others are important only to local residents. All contribute to the economic vitality and outstanding scenic quality of our state.

Unfortunately, unsightly development projects are eroding the scenic beauty of much of Virginia. Some are so large scale, such as power plants or interstate transmission lines, that the major decisions will be

> **Nothing except love is so universally appealing as a view.**
>
> Historian Kenneth Clark

made at the federal and state level. However, local officials can influence the design and siting of these facilities through local land use controls as well as participation in state and federal review procedures. Unquestionably, though, for the bulk of development proposed throughout Virginia—housing, shopping centers, office parks, truck stops and the like—the decision rests almost exclusively with local government. Here cities, towns and counties can take positive action to protect the scenic views and vistas that are a source of community pride and which enhance local economies. What is scenic today will not stay scenic tomorrow by accident.

This publication describes many measures that can be taken to protect visual resources. These include:
- Controlling the size, height and number of outdoor signs
- Prohibiting the construction of new off-premise billboards
- Co-locating or disguising cellular communication towers
- Discouraging ridge-top development
- Undergrounding utility wires
- Placing conservation easements on scenic properties
- Developing design guidelines for chain stores and franchises
- Designating roads as Virginia Scenic Byways

THINGS YOU SHOULD KNOW:

- Numerous studies show that housing, hotels, and offices with scenic views command premium prices. The better the view, the higher the price.

- A 1995 survey of Blue Ridge Parkway users showed that non-resident Parkway visitors contributed more than $403 million in direct expenditures to the counties adjacent to the parkway. These expenditures generated approximately $42 million in state and local tax revenues. Local businesses received an additional $500 million in indirect and induced sales for a total economic impact of more than $904 million per year.

- The President's Commission on Americans Outdoors found that, next to walking, driving for pleasure and sightseeing were Americans' favorite outdoor recreation activities.

- The President's Commission also found that "natural beauty" was the single most important factor in Americans' choice of places to visit for outdoor recreation.

- An analysis of two proposed scenic routes in New Hampshire found that designation of the routes would substantially increase tourism. The U.S. Travel Data Center estimates that scenic byways generate $33,000 per mile in increased consumer spending yearly.

- In Vermont, where billboards have been prohibited since 1975, the tourism industry has benefited tremendously. In fact, the Vermont Chamber of Commerce says, "Although there was some initial sensitivity that removing billboards might hurt tourism, it has had the opposite effect. Tourism is up for all businesses big and small."

- Likewise, the Maine Department of Tourism says, "We have no commercial signs on Interstates. People say they can see the state now. Our mail shows that there is a great deal of appreciation for the fact that we've removed billboards. The initial concern that business would be hurt has been completely unfounded."

- Dozens of communities and two states—North Carolina and South Carolina—have enacted laws to restrict the height of buildings constructed on mountain ridges. Known as Mountain Protection Acts, the laws preserve views of the Appalachian Mountains. Local officials and legislators supported this legislation because they realized that both tourism and second-home construction would benefit from preserving the visual integrity of mountains and ridge lines.

- Smithfield has established a model Community Appearance Commission. Contact: Smithfield Town Manager; (757) 365-4200.

- In Rockbridge County, a conservation easement protects the visible higher elevations of Jump Mountain, a prominent Valley landmark. Parcels at the foot of the mountain were sold to help finance the purchase. The land was so attractive that these sold by word of mouth.

- In James City County, a dedicated funding source of one cent on the real estate tax rate has allowed the

Jump Mountain, Rockbridge County

county to acquire 20 acres of scenic easements along the Colonial Parkway, as well as house lots at the entrance to Jamestown.

FOR MORE INFORMATION:

Aesthetics, Community Character, and the Law, PAS Report #489/490, American Planning Association, 2000; (312) 786-6344.

The Impact of Aesthetics on the Economy and Quality of Life in Virginia and its Localities, Interim Report of the Advisory Commission on Intergovernmental Relations, House Document No. 90, 1998; (804) 786-6508.

The Legal Landscape: Guidelines for Regulating Environmental and Aesthetic Quality, Richard Smardon and James Karp, Van Nostrand Reinbold, New York, NY, 1993.

O, Say, Can You See: A Visual Awareness Tool Kit for Communities, by Scenic America, Washington, DC, 1999; (202) 543-6200.

Scenic Virginia, P.O. Box 17606, Richmond, VA 23226; (804) 288-5817.

Fit Rural Buildings to Their Context

Single-lot development will always be part of the new construction that occurs in Virginia. In rural areas,

New house sited below ridge line

A new house in the Shenandoah Valley that respects local architectural traditions

however, a wide-open landscape can be irreparably changed for the worse by the jarring intrusion of a single poorly sited, highly visible and obviously non-farm building.

Here are some concepts to consider to ensure that new houses or other rural buildings do not diminish the state's natural assets.

Be a Good Steward:
- Protect the primary natural and cultural features of the site
- Keep buildings below the ridge or tree line
- Use traditional materials and roof lines
- Use muted colors
- Maintain existing natural vegetation
- Preserve historic landscape features
- Site driveway unobtrusively
- Hide the garage
- Consider building in town or other close-in location

FOR MORE INFORMATION:

Design with Nature, by Ian McHarg, available from American Planning Association; (312) 786-6344.

"Using Vernacular Architecture in New Home Design," by James W. Wentling, *Development Magazine,* Vol. 8, No. 2, National Association of Home Builders, Fall 1995; (202) 822-0200.

Protect Riparian Areas and Special Habitats

Which stream is more likely to have healthy aquatic habitat?

L AND THAT LIES along rivers, streams, the Chesapeake Bay, and the Atlantic Ocean is important for many reasons. Protecting these fragile coastal and riparian areas offers multiple benefits for people, wildlife, water quality, and the economy.

Riparian areas include floodplains, wetlands, and stream banks. All across Virginia, water courses are abundant. Small, swift creeks flow off the mountains, becoming larger streams, most of which meander through the rolling terrain of the Shenandoah Valley and the Piedmont, and eventually widen through the Tidewater region on their way to the Chesapeake Bay. Rivers like the Shenandoah, the Potomac, the Rappahannock, the York, the James, the Maury, and the New—all give distinctive character to the state and provide abundant natural, scenic, and recreational resources.

Trees, shrubs, and grasses growing along our water courses stabilize stream banks and reduce floodwater velocity. Protected riparian areas also help intercept pollutants and sediment that otherwise would be carried into the stream.

> *A river is more than an amenity. It is a treasure. It offers a necessity of life that must be rationed among those who have power over it.*
>
> Oliver Wendell Holmes

Erosion and stormwater runoff cost money in lost soil and in pollution clean-up. Protection of riparian vegetation is a simple, cost-effective way to save money and protect water quality in the long run.

Ideally, subdivision lines should be drawn so that stream banks are buffered with dedicated open space that protects water quality, wildlife habitat, and other riparian resources while also enhancing property values and reducing the likelihood of flood damage.

Look at the before and after pictures on this page. Clearly the stream on the left, which is typical of the streambeds in many parts of the state, will now send much less soil and pollution downstream.

THINGS YOU SHOULD KNOW:

- In the 2000 Chesapeake Bay Agreement, Virginia agreed to expand public access points to the Bay and its tributaries by 30% over ten years.

- About 66% of Virginia's land—more than 20,000

square miles—is contained within the watershed of the Chesapeake Bay.

- Since colonial times, 42% of Virginia's wetlands have been lost. Through the 1980s, 2,500 acres were lost annually in Virginia's Chesapeake Bay watershed.

- The Commonwealth of Virginia has committed to reducing nitrogen and phosphorus pollution into the Bay by 40%. This will require effort by all citizens of the state.

- Forested areas next to rivers and streams provide a buffer that protects water quality and aquatic habitat.

- Forested riparian buffers can remove 95% of sediment, 80% of nitrogen, and 78% of phosphorus.

- Virginia has set a goal of establishing 610 miles of riparian forest buffers by the year 2010.

- In 1998, riparian plantings were established along 34.5 miles of stream bank in Augusta County. The county has already exceeded its 40% pollution reduction goal.

- In 1998, the Virginia General Assembly defined wetlands and riparian buffers as special classifications of real estate that qualify for local tax exemption, if protected by a perpetual easement.

South River Preserve in Augusta County protects many rare species.

- USDA's Conservation Reserve Program will make annual payments to farmers who protect riparian areas.

- Virginia ranks in the top 10 among all states in globally rare plants and animals.

- The value of all fish caught in fresh and saltwater in Virginia in 1998 was nearly $71 million.

- The Rappahannock-Rapidan Watershed Partnership in Fredericksburg is working to reduce runoff on a 90-acre development, implement best management practices on farmland and reach agreement on a plan to dismantle a dam on the Rappahannock River.

FOR MORE INFORMATION:

Non-Point Source Pollution: A Handbook for Local Governments, PAS Report #476, American Planning Association; (312) 786-6344.

Site Planning for Urban Stream Protection, Metropolitan Washington Council of Governments, 1995; (202) 962-3200.

Local offices of the Virginia Department of Forestry or the USDA Natural Resource Conservation Service.

Cook's Creek Arboretum, Town of Bridgewater

Plant and Preserve Trees

Which street would you rather live on? Which street has higher property values? Which street has lower utility bills?

MANY PARTS OF VIRGINIA are still green and leafy places. However, the trees and woodlands that help give our state its special sense of place are slowly disappearing. Gypsy moths, air pollution, careless cutting, utility companies, highway widening, and new development are all combining to rob Virginia of its age-old trees.

THINGS YOU SHOULD KNOW:

■ Trees are good for business. According to the National Association of Home Builders, developed lots with trees sell for an average of 20-30 percent more than similar lots without trees. Mature trees that are preserved during development add more value to a lot than post-construction landscaping. Tree planting and preservation pay off not only on upscale properties, but also on small, inexpensive lots.

■ Saving and relocating 3,000 mature trees on the site of the University of Virginia's research park cost 50 percent less than removing the trees and planting new ones—plus there was no wait for the saplings to grow.

■ Trees are also good for the environment. Trees lower cooling costs. As a homeowner, your utility bills will go up when trees go down. In addition, electrical plants will burn more fuel, adding to air pollution.

■ Trees play a major role in slowing soil erosion and stormwater runoff. A study of Atlanta by American Forests found a 20% increase in stormwater runoff in areas where trees were replaced with development.

What Virginia communities can do:

• Plant more new trees, especially shade trees along streets, roads, and in riparian areas.

• Promote the protection of existing trees, particularly during the development process.

In my travels throughout the country, I see so many new suburbs utterly denuded of trees; ironic since the new owners' first instinct is to plant as many trees as possible. My advice, leave the original trees. It's good for business and very good for the environment.

Former President George Bush

Examples of Tree Preservation

Trees can be saved during development of all types. The benefits of such efforts are shown by these local examples.

Residents of houses with full tree canopies enjoy lower utility bills.

Even modest subdivisions, like this mobile home park in Rockingham County, can have a pleasant environment if trees are retained.

Majestic trees, carefully preserved during construction, now shade the swimming pool of the new Hampton Inn in Lexington.

Retaining "tree save zones" along commercial corridors greatly reduces the visual impact of new development.

This unusual deodar cedar was saved when a new office was constructed in Staunton.

- Encourage or require the landscaping of parking lots and commercial areas.

- Recognize, honor, and reward individuals and companies who take the lead in planting and protecting trees.

- Enact a local tree preservation ordinance.

- Have your community apply to the National Arbor Day Foundation for a Tree City USA Designation, as have Winchester, Staunton, Waynesboro, Falls Church, and other communities.

- Have your community apply to the Virginia Department of Forestry for an Urban and Community Forestry grant to fund projects such as tree planting, tree care workshops or community forestry initiatives.

FOR MORE INFORMATION:

Building Greener Neighborhoods: Trees As Part of the Plan, by American Forests and the National Association of Home Builders, Washington, DC, 1995; (202) 822-0200.

Falls Church Tree Conservation Ordinance, Falls Church, Virginia. This Virginia community has an outstanding tree planting and protection program and an excellent landscaping ordinance; (703) 248-5003.

Tree Conservation Ordinances, by Christopher Duerkson, PAS Report #446, 1993, American Planning Association Planners Book Service; (312) 786-6344.

Trees Are Treasure: Sustaining the Community Forest, 1993. A video on the benefits of preserving trees in commercial and residential developments. Contact Scenic America, Washington, DC; (202) 543-6200.

Virginia Department of Forestry, Fontaine Research Park, 900 Natural Resources Drive, Suite 800, Charlottesville, VA 22903; (804) 977-6555.

Conserve Natural and Scenic Assets

Cutting down trees can reduce property values.

Grow In, Not Out

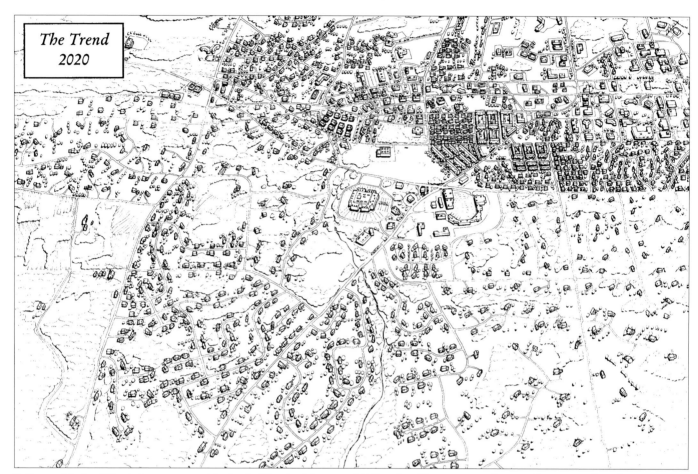

The Trend 2020

What will the Virginia countryside look like in 20 years? Like the illustration above, if current development trends continue.

Virginia is going to grow; the only real question is where and how will this growth occur. Maintaining the character and livability of Virginia communities will require keeping rural areas rural while encouraging new development in existing towns, cities, and older suburbs. In other words—grow in, not out.

As a healthy, expanding state, we can expect many new enterprises and residents in the coming years. How we

Illustrations from *Landscapes: Managing Change in Chester County 1996-2020,* Comprehensive Planning Element, 1996. Rerinted with permission of the Chester County Planning Commission, West Chester, PA.

accommodate these new homes and businesses will help determine the quality of life for all of us and for future generations.

The illustrations above make the choice clear. Left unchecked, current patterns of sprawling, leapfrog development will make our beautiful state a featureless blur that is neither town nor country.

The alternative is to encourage growth into cohesive, walkable communities, small and large, and to shape and design growth in rural areas so that it fits the rural setting. A more compact development pattern can accommodate the same amount of growth while benefiting both town and countryside.

There is growing recognition that keeping development compact is better than allowing scattered low-density development in the countryside. This is

Accomplishing this goal, however, is one of the nation's toughest planning challenges because current public policies often make it easier and cheaper to develop in the countryside, and local governments have limited resources and inadequate tools for addressing the

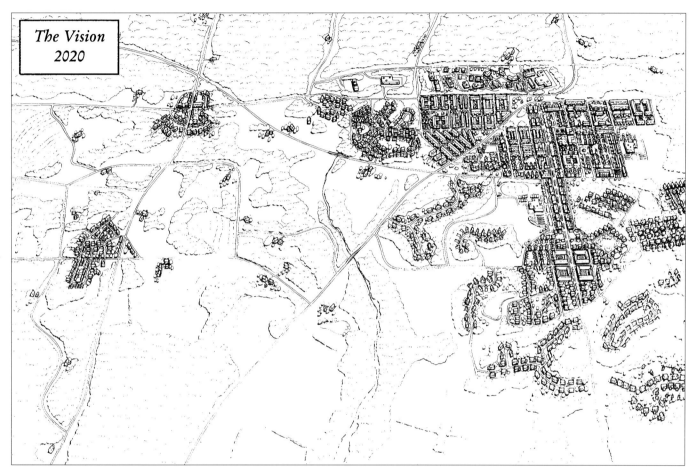

The Vision 2020

This alternative pattern accommodates the same amount of growth while preserving the countryside.

because scatter-shot development has a profound impact on issues as diverse as water quality, traffic congestion, economic development, and open space preservation. By channeling growth to existing urban and suburban areas, we can reduce our footprint on the landscape, preserve open space—and save money on public facilities too.

Almost without exception, county comprehensive plans throughout Virginia express a desire to maintain rural character and to channel growth into planned service areas. At the same time, cities and towns are trying to encourage growth within their borders.

issue. Yet no rural protection effort can work unless people find attractive and desirable places to live in the areas designated for growth.

The Grow In, Grow Out Quiz

For each major new development in your community, the following questions can be asked:

- Is the location appropriate?
- Does the siting respect the landscape context?
- Does the layout maintain a clear edge between urban and rural?
- Do building designs reflect regional character and traditions, or otherwise suit the site?

- Are there costs to the community—subsidies, infrastructure, public services, environmental or social costs?
- Do the benefits to the community outweigh the costs?

Economic Advantages of Curtailing Sprawl:

- Lower service costs
- Full use of the investment in existing water, sewer, roads, and other infrastructure
- Potential to plan efficient expansion of services
- Delay or avoidance of new infrastructure investment
- Lower per unit costs
- Less money spent on fuel and transportation
- Less time spent in cars
- Less money spent on roads
- Lower school construction costs
- Opportunity for heritage tourism
- Potential to attract higher-caliber employers

There is a direct connection between suburban sprawl and the spiraling costs of government.

James Howard Kunstler,
Geography of Nowhere

FOR MORE INFORMATION:

Alternatives to Sprawl, by Dwight Young, 1995, Lincoln Institute of Land Policy, Cambridge, MA; (800) 526-3873.

Beyond Sprawl: Land Management Techniques to Protect the Chesapeake Bay, Chesapeake Bay Program, U.S. Environmental Protection Agency, 1997, Document #EPA 903-B-97-005; (800) 968-7229 (free).

Once There Were Greenfields: How Urban Sprawl is Undermining America's Environment, Economy and Social Fabric, by Kaid Benfield et. al., Natural Resources Defense Council, Washington, DC, 20005, 1999; (202) 289-6868.

Sprawl Costs Us All! A Guide to the Costs of Suburban Sprawl and How to Create Livable Communities in Virginia, A Sierra Club Report, September 1997, Sierra Club, 69 Franklin Street, Annapolis, MD 21401; (410) 268-7411.

Who Pays for Sprawl? The Economic, Social, and Environmental Impacts of Sprawl Development: A Literature Review, Chesapeake Bay Program, U.S. Environmental Protection Agency, 1998. Document EPA 903-R-98-011; (800) 968-7229 (free).

What Is Sprawl?

Sprawl is characterized by

- Low-density housing and commercial development
- Unlimited outward expansion from the city center
- Leapfrog development
- Fragmented government control over land use
- Dominance of the car for transportation
- Segregation of land uses
- Disappearing open space on the urban fringe

Adapted from: Anthony Downs, *New Visions for Metropolitan America*

Northern Virginia traffic jam: Is this the future we want for all of Virginia?

Understand the Costs of Sprawl

Which will generate more in net income for a community: a working farm or a new residential subdivision far from town?

ALTHOUGH MOST VIRGINIANS "know it when they see it," sprawl is often difficult to define. However, sprawl is typically characterized by low densities, a segregation of uses and housing types (i.e., houses in one place, apartments in another place, stores and offices somewhere else, etc.), travel dominated by motor vehicles, disappearing farmland and open space, and continuous commercial strip development dominated by signs and asphalt parking lots. While there's no denying that some aspects of sprawl—for example, large yards or convenient parking—are valued by many Virginians, there's also no denying that sprawl imposes many costs on the Commonwealth.

At least 500 costs-of-sprawl studies have been completed nationwide, including statewide studies in Rhode Island, New Jersey, Pennsylvania, California, Maine, and New Hampshire. These studies confirm that sprawl imposes costs on taxpayers, citizens, and local governments in at least five different ways.

First, these studies show that sprawl typically increases the costs to build and maintain roads and schools. For example, at least three major research investigations

There are alternatives to sprawl that are more attractive, efficient and profitable.

Ed McMahon,
The Conservation Fund

have concluded that planned growth scenarios that avoid sprawl can lower construction costs for roads, utilities, and schools by up to 25 percent.

Second, sprawl diminishes quality of life by increasing the concentration of poorer citizens in urban areas and by creating a lack of affordable housing in the suburbs where job growth is greatest.

Third, sprawl erodes farmlands, natural areas, and open spaces, particularly at the suburban fringe. Virginia lost more than 467,000 acres of farmland, forest, and open space in just five years between 1992 and 1997, and the rate of agricultural land loss has accelerated in recent years. One reason is that the average lot size in Virginia has been increasing at the same time that average household size has been decreasing.

Fourth, sprawl also leads to increased air and water pollution. For example, a study by the Chesapeake Bay Commission in 1997 found that air quality could be significantly improved by reducing the growth rate of vehicle miles traveled. Likewise, sprawl contributes to polluted stormwater runoff which eventually ends up in Virginia's rivers and the Chesapeake Bay.

Finally, studies say sprawl contributes to greater personal stress because it forces people to spend more and more time in their cars and less and less time with their families or on other more fulfilling endeavors. For example, a 1990 study found that traffic congestion had a statistically significant effect on job satisfaction, work absences due to illness, and overall incidents of colds and flu. The study also found stress to be strongly associated with freeway travel and road rage, both of which increase with low-density, dispersed development patterns.

THINGS YOU SHOULD KNOW:

Fiscal Costs

- The New Jersey State Development Plan estimated that, over a 20-year period, infrastructure for sprawl-type development would cost $1.3 billion more to build and $112 million more annually to service than would accommodating the same population in a more compact pattern.

- A study by the American Farmland Trust found that if California's Central Valley chooses compact growth over sprawl, it could save $29 billion in taxpayer-financed services over 50 years.

- A study by the Chesapeake Bay Program found that choosing compact development over sprawl could save $10.8 billion in road construction in the Chesapeake Bay region over a 30-year period.

- A Prince William County study found that even with the highest property tax rate in Virginia, the cost of providing services to new subdivisions results in a $1,688 shortfall for each new home.

Social Costs

- Virginians are spending more and more time behind the wheel of a car. The average commute is getting longer, and sprawling development patterns force people to drive everywhere for everything.

- More suburban teenagers now die from auto accidents than inner city teenagers die from gunshot wounds.

- Fewer and fewer children can walk to school in Virginia because new suburban schools are always in far-flung locations accessible only by school bus or car.

- Loudoun County, now the fastest growing county in Virginia, recently announced that it would have to build "cheaper schools" with fewer amenities because of rapidly escalating school construction costs.

- The American Association of Retired Persons (AARP) says, "the overwhelming number of older persons desire to remain in their current homes and communities," but this is becoming harder to accomplish because many older people are unable to drive.

Environmental Costs

- Between 1982 and 1997, Virginia lost 920,800 acres of farmland and forest to development.

- An American Lung Association report on discouraging sprawl stated, "land use policy is crucial to controlling air pollution."

- Air pollution has dramatically reduced visibility from the Skyline Drive and Blue Ridge Parkway over the last decade.

- An acre of parking lot generates 16 times more runoff than an acre of meadow.

- The health of the Chesapeake Bay is threatened by non-point-source pollution, much of which is generated by runoff from roads and parking lots.

Techniques for Maintaining a Clear Edge

COMMUNITIES AROUND THE COUNTRY are using a variety of techniques to maintain a clear edge between town and countryside. Here are some of the most common techniques:

Urban Growth Boundaries

An urban growth boundary is a planning tool that establishes a dividing line between areas appropriate for urban development and areas appropriate for rural or agricultural uses. Every city and town in Oregon has established an urban growth boundary. So have many communities in California and Washington. Here in the East, urban growth boundaries are being used in places like Lexington, Kentucky, and Lancaster County, Pennsylvania. For more information contact: Lancaster County Planning Commission, 50 N. Duke Street, Lancaster, PA 17068; (717) 299-8333.

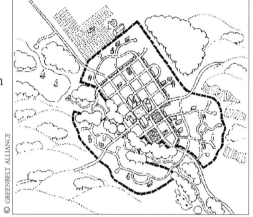

Urban growth boundary

© GREENBELT ALLIANCE

Development Service Districts

Some Virginia communities have established the equivalent of urban growth boundaries by designating "development service districts," which map in advance those areas where a county will accept responsibility for providing infrastructure. For example, Albemarle County has had designated growth areas since 1971. Isle of Wight County established development service districts in its 1991 Comprehensive Plan, and Frederick County has established boundaries beyond which water and sewer lines may not be extended. Targeting growth in and around these areas can help to prevent sprawling development in other areas of the county. For more information contact: Albemarle County, Department of Planning, 401 McIntire Road, Charlottesville, VA 22903; (804) 296-5823.

Greenbelts

Many communities have invested in open space to create greenbelts. Boulder, Colorado, for example, is surrounded by a 31,000-acre "greenbelt" of public open space and mountain parks. The greenbelt began in 1967 when voters approved an additional third of a cent sales tax for open space. Closer to home, Maryland has a Rural Historic Villages Program which has created greenbelts around a number of small towns such as Sharpsburg, Burkittsville, and Claiborne. These greenbelts were created by purchasing development rights on surrounding farmland. For more information contact: Maryland Environmental Trust, 100 Community Place, 1st Floor, Crownsville, MD 21032-2032; (410) 514-7900.

Smart Growth Laws

Smart growth laws use the state or local government budget process to encourage growth in areas already served by existing infrastructure. For example, the state of Maryland does not prohibit development in the countryside, but as a result of its new Smart Growth Act, it will no longer pay for roads, schools or other public improvements outside of designated "smart growth areas." Likewise, the City of Lancaster, California, allows developers to build wherever they want—as long as they pay a premium for building farther from town. For more information contact: Maryland Office of Planning, 301 West Preston Street, Suite 1101, Baltimore, MD 21201; (410) 767-4500.

Encourage Infill Development

Does it make more sense to build on greenfield sites or to encourage development on vacant lots, overlooked parcels or abandoned properties in existing communities?

VIRGINIA IS DEVELOPING LAND at a much faster rate than our population growth. While development at the edge of a community undoubtedly represents new investment, it also accounts for substantial long-term public costs. According to a report by the U.S. Office of Technology Assessment, a single home built on the urban fringe requires $10,000 more in public services than one built in the urban core.

One alternative to land consumptive suburban sprawl is to encourage more infill development. This makes more efficient use of public and private infrastructure by putting additional people where roads, schools, sewers, and water lines already exist.

This does not mean overcrowding; in fact, many of Virginia's cities, towns, and older suburbs have lost population in recent decades—so there are many opportunities for infill development on vacant lots, overlooked parcels, or abandoned properties, including brownfields or former industrial sites.

There are at least half a million brownfield sites in the United States, including many in Virginia. While liabil-

Bringing market rate housing back to the cities is critical to any effort to revitalize the nation's cities.

National Association of Homebuilders

ity concerns have long been a deterrent to brownfield redevelopment, many states have adopted voluntary clean-up programs which are generating renewed interest in the redevelopment of lightly contaminated property. Many developers know that it is now possible to reap substantial profits from these contaminated lands—turning brownfields into greenbacks.

Advantages of Infill Development:

- Uses existing roads and utilities
- Convenient location
- Certainty of development pattern
- Cultural facilities, parks, and other amenities
- Cost savings for developers and residents

Financial benefits of infill development can be great. Using existing utilities and infrastructure can reduce costs. For buildings that are historic, considerable federal and state tax incentives are offered for rehabilitation. Local enterprise zones and other programs also can provide incentives for investment. An often overlooked advantage of investing in an infill site is the certainty provided by a mature development pattern and known neighbors.

Creative and attractive infill projects can be found throughout Virginia. For example, the Ghent neighborhood in Norfolk includes a delightful mix of both old and new houses and apartments. Likewise, the Village at Cornwall near downtown Leesburg is a development of architecturally compatible new houses within walking distance of shopping and schools. Potomac

A Winchester property swap kept major offices downtown.

New office building in Old Town Alexandria

Yard in Alexandria and Arlington is a 240-acre brownfields project on the site of the former RF&P Railroad yard that is being developed with a mix of residential, retail, and office uses.

THINGS YOU SHOULD KNOW:

■ To encourage development near transit stops, Fannie Mae started a pilot program offering "location-

efficient mortgages." The program enables buyers who purchase homes near transit lines to qualify for larger mortgages, since they no longer have to spend as much on personal transportation.

■ Inner-city residents have far more money to spend than stores in which to spend it, according to the U.S. Housing and Urban Development Department (HUD). In 48 cities studied, retail sales were $8.7 billion less than residents' buying power.

A new motel on Main Street in Charlottesville

■ Downtowns across America are reporting a strong increase in people choosing to live in center city neighborhoods, townhouses, and loft apartments. The prime reasons for this are that crime is down, traffic congestion is up, and there are more amenities closer in.

■ The National Association of Homebuilders, in partnership with HUD and the U.S. Conference of Mayors, has announced the goal of constructing one million additional market-rate housing units in the nation's cities and inner-ring suburbs by 2010.

■ Arlington County has done an outstanding job of encouraging high-quality infill development. Wilson Boulevard between Ballston and Rosslyn, once an aging, low-density retail strip, is now the county's main commercial area with a pedestrian-friendly mix of offices, retail, and housing.

- Wal-Mart recently invested in downtown Rutland, Vermont, reusing an old Kmart building and sharing parking with neighbors.

- Culpeper has a new multi-screen movie theater that was constructed on a vacant downtown lot.

- In Winchester, a three-way property swap among Frederick County, the city, and F&M Bank kept key offices downtown and benefited all parties. The county expanded its offices on former bank property, while the bank rehabilitated the county's former office building. Each gained more convenient and suitable space, while the city, which donated parking, enjoys increased property values and the presence of office workers that keep downtown strong.

- Charlottesville's Kellytown infill project is a traditional neighborhood development designed cooperatively by the builder and the neighborhood association. It provides 32 new houses and the right to add 10 additional accessory living units. Despite being on small, narrow lots, the traditional-style houses with access to a preserved forested stream valley are selling—at up to twice the expected price. Contact Charlottesville Planning Director, (804) 970-3182.

Arlington County is Virginia's leader in high-quality infill development.

- For example, within a third of a mile of Arlington County's Ballston Metro Station are two universities, two public schools, the county's main library, three hotels, recreational facilities, a retirement community, a regional mall, and many corporate headquarters including FDIC, Quest, Inc., and The Nature Conservancy. On the edges of this "new downtown" are stable residential neighborhoods.

- By contrast, within a third of a mile of Fairfax County's Vienna Metro Station are large parking lots, 200 acres of vacant land, a townhouse development and a few single-family houses.

Infill development surrounding Arlington County's Ballston Metro Station

Area surrounding Fairfax County's Vienna Metro Station

FOR MORE INFORMATION:

Building Livable Communities: A Policymaker's Guide to Infill Development, The Center for Livable Communities, Local Government Commission, 1414 K Street, Suite 250, Sacramento, CA 95814; (916) 448-1198.

Developing Infill Housing in Inner-City Neighborhoods, by Diane Suchman, Urban Land Institute, 1997; (800) 321-5011.

Turning Brownfields into Greenbacks, by Robert A. Simons, Urban Land Institute, 1998; (800) 321-5011.

Use Open Space Development Techniques

Suppose you were a developer with 200 acres. Which do you think would be more profitable:
a development with 100 two-acre lots and no open space, or a development with 100 one-acre lots
and 100 acres of open space?

COMMUNITIES ACROSS VIRGINIA are realizing that they can conserve their special open spaces and natural resources at the same time they achieve their development objectives.

Subdivisions in rural areas are not encouraged. But if a rural location is selected, there are still ways to protect the rural landscape by carefully planning the new development.

Each time a property is subdivided, an opportunity exists for adding land to a community-wide network of open space. Conservation design simply rearranges the development on each parcel so that half (or more) of the buildable land is set aside as open space. This allows the same number of houses to be built in a less land consumptive manner, allowing the balance of the property to be protected and added to a network of community green space. The density neutral approach outlined below is a fair and equitable way to balance conservation and development.

Open space or cluster developments can be more profitable than conventional developments. They can also minimize the loss of farmland and forest while increasing property values. These subdivisions provide the same number of dwelling units as conventional development. They are carefully designed, however, to preserve parts of a rural site and cluster the houses on the remainder.

Many counties in Virginia and elsewhere require "clustering"; others allow it as an option in their rural areas. Open space developments can be a profitable option for small-scale subdivisions. They can blend houses into the landscape and to some degree can allow for the continuation of working farms.

It is important to recognize that while open space subdivisions provide many benefits for people, wildlife and the economy, they cannot replace the need for a solid policy of farmland and rural area protection or the need for close-in, mixed-use communities.

What is Open Space Design?

Look at the drawings that follow. The first one shows a Virginia farm before development. The next shows a residential subdivision that is common throughout Virginia. The entire tract is subdivided into houses and streets. The final one shows an open space development that contains the same number of houses but preserves more than half the site as open space.

Open Space Site Design

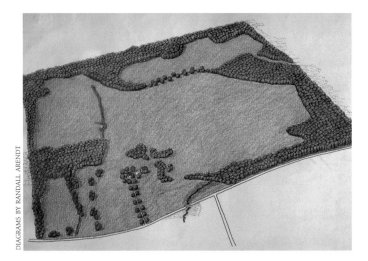

Virginia farm before development

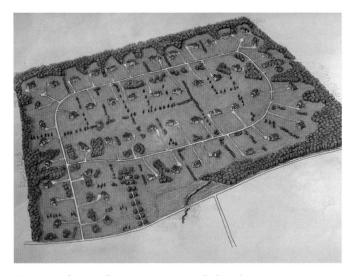

Virginia farm after conventional development

Virginia farm after open space development

What Are the Advantages of Open Space Development?

■ Developers save money by not having to build as many streets, gutters, drains, or sidewalks.

■ Studies show that people will pay more for houses that are bordered by open space.

■ Many people prefer open space developments because they provide access to nature and outdoor recreation, enhance property values, and reduce the time and expense of maintaining extra- large yards.

■ A majority of homeowners in golf course developments do not play golf. They say they like to live next to protected green space.

■ The public benefits because open space developments mean less concrete and asphalt, less polluted runoff, more wildlife habitat, and more trees and green space.

How Do We Make Open Space Development Happen?

Better development occurs in two basic ways: (1) by increasing the market demand for open space development and (2) by changing zoning ordinances to permit and encourage these developments.

Developers, like all business people, respond to market demand. Look, for example, at what is happening in Arlington County. There is a growing demand for housing with access to the Washington area's Metro system, and developers are eagerly responding. Likewise, as the demand for open space development grows, we will start to see more such developments.

The second way is to change zoning ordinances to make it easier to build open space developments. Because of the current emphasis on large- lot zoning with wide setbacks, many ordinances now discourage these developments.

THINGS YOU SHOULD KNOW:

- A 1995 nationwide survey of prospective home buyers conducted for a group of large-volume home builders found that consumers rated "lots of natural open space" as an "extremely important" feature in new residential development. In fact, open space rated second overall out of 40 possible features.

- In its designated rural areas, Fauquier County requires that 85 percent of the land be permanently protected. A variety of subdivisions have been built to these standards.

- Isle of Wight County requires preservation of 50 percent of land in its Rural Preservation District.

- Many zoning ordinances and maps allow for more residential and commercial development than can be supported, thus encouraging sprawling development patterns.

- A National Association of Home Builders comparison of a conventional layout versus a clustered layout with 20 percent preserved open space found that the open space design cut development costs by one third.

- A study of home values in two subdivisions that are nearly identical except that one reserved 50% of the site as open space found that the clustered homes appreciated 12.7 percent more than those in the conventional subdivision, despite having smaller lots.

- The Maryland Planning Office estimates that the same housing density accommodated on one-acre lots saves approximately $3,500 per lot in development costs compared to five-acre lots.

The Conservation Design Concept

In his book *Growing Greener: Putting Conservation into Local Codes,* land use expert Randall Arendt explains how open space design works.

Designing subdivisions around the central organizing principle of land conservation is not difficult. However, it is essential that ordinances contain clear standards to guide the conservation design process. The four-step approach described below has proven to be effective in laying out new full-density developments where all the significant natural and cultural features have been preserved.

Step One consists of identifying the land that should

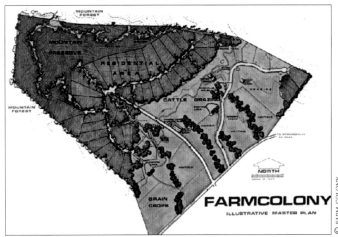

The master plan for Farmcolony in Greene County clusters homes to protect farmland and the mountain background, as shown in the photo and map above.

Wintergreen in Nelson County clusters homes to preserve natural areas.

be permanently protected. The developer performs a detailed site analysis in order to precisely locate features to be conserved. The developer first identifies all the constrained areas, such as wetlands, floodplains, and steep slopes, called Primary Conservation Areas. The developer then identifies Secondary Conservation Areas, which comprise noteworthy features of the property that are typically unprotected under current codes: mature woodlands, greenways and trails, river and stream corridors, prime farmland, hedgerows and individual free-standing trees or tree groups, wildlife habitats and travel corridors, historic sites and structures, scenic viewsheds, etc. After "greenlining" these conservation elements, the remaining part of the property becomes the Potential Development Area.

Step Two involves locating sites of individual houses within the Potential Development Area so that their views of the open space are maximized. The number of houses is a function of the density permitted within the zoning district.

Step Three simply involves "connecting the dots" with streets and informal trails, while **Step Four** consists of drawing in the lot lines.

This approach reverses the sequence of steps in laying out conventional subdivisions, where the street system is the first thing to be identified, followed by lot lines

fanning out to encompass every square foot of ground into houselots. When municipalities require nothing more than "houselots and streets," that is all they receive. But by setting community standards higher and requiring significant open space as a precondition for achieving full density, officials can effectively encourage conservation subdivision design. The protected land in each new subdivision would then become building blocks that add new acreage to community-wide networks of interconnected open space each time a property is developed.

FOR MORE INFORMATION:

Conservation Design for Subdivisions, by Randall Arendt, Island Press, 1996; (800) 828-1302.

Growing Greener: Putting Conservation Into Local Plans and Ordinances, by Randall Arendt, Island Press, 1999; (800) 828-1302.

Preserving Rural Character, by Fred Heyer, PAS Report # 429, 1990, American Planning Association; (312) 786-6344.

Rural Areas Land Use Plan, Fauquier County, Virginia, December 1995, Department of Community Development, (540) 347-8703.

Rural By Design, by Randall Arendt with Elizabeth Brabec, Harry Dodson, Christine Reid, and Robert Yaro, 1994, American Planning Association; (312) 786-6344.

Delineate Gateways

Which gateway makes a better first impression? Which community looks like one in which you would rather spend time and money?

FIRST IMPRESSIONS ARE IMPORTANT to communities. Just as with meeting a person, a good first impression can make a difference. A bad first impression is hard to change. The gateway into a community is like its "front door." It provides the introduction to a community. It can either express a community's pride and sense of place or it can give a community a poor public image.

Compare the photos of the community gateways on this and the following page. Then ask yourself the following questions:

Which gateway makes a better first impression?
Which one looks like a community with a sense of pride?
Which community looks like one in which you would rather spend time and money?
Which one looks more like the gateway into your community?

Many parts of a town or community have boundaries drawn around them. These boundaries usually exist in people's minds. They mark the end of one kind of activity or one kind of place and the beginning of another. In many cases, a community can be made more memorable, more vivid, more alive if the bound-

ary that exists in people's minds also exists physically on the ground. In rural areas, gateways provide an area of transition between town and countryside; in urban areas they help mark the boundaries between one community and another.

THINGS YOU SHOULD KNOW:

- Gateways can provide information to tourists by directing them to areas of interest and by providing clues to the historical, cultural, and economic foundation of an area.

- Major gateways to Virginia include the Interstate corridors—I-81, I-95, I-64, and I-66. Tourists, new residents, and potential investors all form their first impressions of Virginia along these corridors, and the interstate interchange areas are the front door to many of our communities.

- How we plan and build along the interstate corridors is critical to the character of Virginia communities and the image and economic health of our state.

- As anyone can see, the exceptional beauty and visual quality along Virginia's interstate corridors has deteriorated in recent years. Truck stops, giant signs, gaudy billboards, and look-alike fast food restaurants now dominate many of the interchange areas along I-95 and I-81, in particular, and this is affecting how people perceive our state.

■ A 1992 report by the Interstate-81 Corridor Council expressed it this way: "Each mile of the Western Virginia landscape carries subtle messages to the travelers along Interstate-81 about our economic health, whether we are proud of our heritage, or whether we care about the land."

■ Green space can act as a community separator, delineating where one community begins and another ends. Douglas County, Colorado, for example, has been purchasing land along I-25 to create a permanent buffer between the suburbs of Denver and those of Colorado Springs.

Gateway to Fauquier County

Gateway marred by billboards

Gateway to Staunton

Gateway to Woodstock

Gateway to Edinburg

Gateway to Mt. Jackson

Gateway to Warrenton

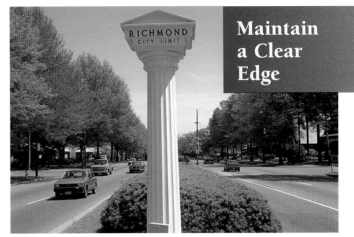

Maintain a Clear Edge

Gateway to Richmond

FOR MORE INFORMATION:

Designing Urban Corridors, PAS Report #418, by Kirk R. Bishop, 1990, American Planning Association Planners Book Service; (312) 786-6344.

"Gateways: Creating a Civic Identity," Suzanne Sutro Rhees, *Planning Commissioners Journal,* No. 21, Winter 1996; (802) 864-9083.

"Planning Basics for Gateway Design," by Michael Barrett, *Zoning News,* American Planning Association; (312) 431-9100.

The Role of Civic Gateways in Promoting Community Image and Use, by Vernon Hustead, Master's Thesis, Morgan State University, Spring 1995; (410) 263-9708.

Enhance Cities, Towns and Villages

If you had a choice, would you rather live in a small town or in suburbia?

THE FLIP SIDE of not developing the countryside is building attractive places to live in the areas where growth is desired and can be accommodated. This means emphasizing quality, not quantity.

People crave a sense of community. Our state's traditional communities come in many different scales. All offer a sense of place, a compact settlement pattern, and proximity to services. They are places where you can know your neighbor and walk to school or the store.

Many of Virginia's cities, small towns, and older suburbs—in places like Arlington, Leesburg, Portsmouth, Richmond, Roanoke, and Winchester—retain a high degree of historic integrity. They are vibrant places to live and work. Some even retain a small-town atmosphere. All of these communities have room to grow from within. They also can be extended in a compatible pattern. It even can be appropriate in some areas to create new hamlets or villages.

> *It is within our power to create places worthy of our affection.*
>
> James Howard Kunstler,
> *Geography of Nowhere*

While most Americans live in suburbs, surveys reveal a strong preference for the "small town" as the ideal place to live. The many villages and small towns sprinkled throughout Virginia are not just charming anachronisms; rather they are models for how we could build in the future. In fact, functional human settlements are almost always made up of a balance of jobs, homes, services, and amenities. Small towns and walkable urban neighborhoods provide many opportunities for redevelopment while offering the conveniences and social advantages of a real community.

One way to bring about compatible growth of villages, towns, and cities is to prepare an area plan. With local community input, the community can set locations for roads and general uses in the core boundaries and in adjoining areas. This planning gives the developer confidence of project approval and assures neighbors that new development will be of compatible character. A plan means greater likelihood that the community vision will be achieved. For the locality, this means less potential for conflict and lawsuits and greater confidence in planning for population growth and needed services.

THINGS YOU SHOULD KNOW:

■ Chesterfield County has developed growth plans for each of its designated villages. This strategy has lessened the acrimony and lawsuits over development and is resulting in higher-quality, more-compatible growth. The Chester Village Plan (construction began in 1998) has been so well received that adjacent property is being developed as a traditional neighborhood development to tie into the new core. Contact Chesterfield County Director of Planning, (804) 748-1040.

■ Shipcarpenter Square in Lewes, Delaware, adds residential units in a way that complements the surrounding rectilinear street pattern of this historic town. Rather than using a suburban-style layout

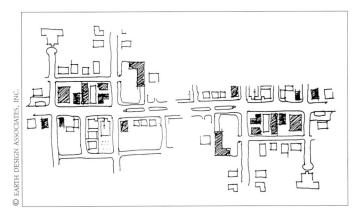

Natural extension of connected streets

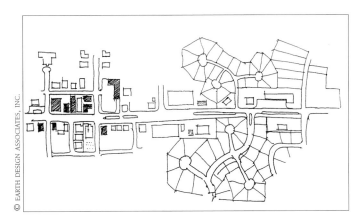

Disconnected "pod" growth

with curvilinear streets and cul-de-sacs, its 36 lots are arranged along a U-shaped street enclosing a 2-acre community green. All of the houses are historic homes rescued from demolition and moved to the site.

New homes on street extending Leesburg's village grid

■ Loudoun County encourages the development of rural hamlets through its zoning ordinance and comprehensive plan. At least 80 percent of the tract must be kept in open space and houses (between 10 and 25) must be oriented to a village green. Contact Loudoun County Planning Director, (703) 777-0246.

FOR MORE INFORMATION:

Reinventing the Village, by Suzanne Sutro, PAS Report #430, American Planning Association, 1990; (312) 786-6344.

Rural By Design, by Randall Arendt with Elizabeth Brabec, Harry Dodson, Christine Reid, and Robert Yaro, 1994, American Planning Association; (312) 786-6344.

Village Planning Handbook, Bucks County Planning Commission, Doylestown, PA 18901; (215) 345-3400.

Design Real Neighborhoods

If you were in the market for a new house, what would be more important to you—the size of the lot or the character of the house and neighborhood?

UILDING LIVEABLE COMMUNITIES means ensuring a convenient mix of the things that meet people's daily needs, including homes, schools, services, and amenities. Traditional neighborhoods historically have offered a place to live for people of all ages and incomes and life stages.

Ideally, these residential settings also are attractive, walkable, and satisfying—places people enjoy. Well-designed communities are not just a collection of individual houses. Unlike conventional subdivisions, neighborhood quality is not based solely on lot size and square footage. Equal attention is paid to creating an inviting public realm conducive to walking, casual socializing, and community function.

What makes a wonderful neighborhood?
* Quality of the public space
* Variety of uses and building types
* Connections—to people and to daily needs
* Places to walk
* Trees and green space

Open space is vital to human well-being, yet many post-World War II subdivisions provide no parks or usable open space. Children have few places to play except the cul-de-sac, and parents are forced to drive their children everywhere for everything, from soccer games to birthday parties.

As communities grow, it is increasingly important to provide parks and open spaces. New developments have the opportunity to include wonderful outdoor spaces. On a small scale, play areas and greens can serve surrounding residences. Greenways can turn undevelopable stream corridors into peaceful areas that maintain natural habitat. These open spaces can be the places of the heart and important community landmarks for the future.

A development trend that holds great hope for building better communities is "traditional neighborhood development" (TND), also known as "new urbanism." More than 200 such projects are underway throughout the nation, including a number in Virginia and adjoining states.

Human settlement patterns—the pattern and density of land use—have profound, in fact controlling, impact on current and longer term economic prosperity, social stability and environmental sustainability.

Ed Risse, Synergy Planning

Common Features of Traditional Neighborhood Development:

• Compact form that encourages walking
• Streetscape designed for pedestrians
• Buildings set close to the sidewalk
• Narrow connected streets
• Neighborhood parks and open spaces
• Mix of housing types and price ranges
• Architecture that reflects the community or region
• Compatible non-residential uses, including schools and neighborhood retail

Common Features of Conventional Development:

• Isolated "pods" of look-alike, single-price-range houses
• Separation from other uses
• Few places to walk
• Lack of parks or open space
• Houses dominated by garages
• Dead-end streets and cul-de-sacs
• No way to get around without a car

Look at the examples on the following pages. Compare these to the features of most modern subdivisions. Which are more liveable?

THINGS YOU SHOULD KNOW:

■ Eighty-six percent of consumers say they would prefer to shop in a village center with a mix of stores and civic buildings rather than a strip shopping center.

■ Today, almost 70% of American households do not have school-aged children. As a result, there is a great need for housing for retirees, empty nesters, single parents, unrelated singles, and other niche markets.

■ Virginia Beach found that traditional neighborhood development would reduce the number of miles driven by approximately 65%.

■ Kentlands, a traditional neighborhood development in Maryland, is so refreshingly pedestrian-oriented that people from surrounding areas drive there to walk for pleasure. In fact, a university study found that home buyers are willing to pay $30,000 to $40,000 more for homes in Kentlands compared to similar homes in the area.

■ Interviews with residents of traditional neighborhood developments have found an even greater sense of community than anticipated. Residents speak of knowing everyone within several blocks.

■ Traditional neighborhood developments can outsell conventional developments. For example, Northwest Landing in Dupont, Washington, is the hottest development in its market, outselling its competition by a margin of nearly two to one.

■ In Minneapolis, every home is within six blocks of a well-kept park.

FOR MORE INFORMATION:

A Better Place to Live: Reshaping the American Suburb, by Philip Langdon, Harper-Collins, New York, NY, 1994.

A Better Way to Grow—For More Livable Communities and a Healthier Chesapeake Bay, by the Chesapeake Bay Foundation, 1996; (804) 780-1392.

"New Urban News," a bimonthly newsletter, P.O. Box 6515, Ithaca, NY 14851; (607) 275-3087.

New Urbanism: Market, Myth and Reality, a video by the Rocky Mountain Institute, 1739 Snowmass Creek Road, Snowmass, CO 81654; (970) 927-3851.

The New Urbanism: Toward an Architecture of Community, by Peter Katz, McGraw-Hill, Inc., New York, NY, 1994.

Mix Uses and Building Types in New Developments

Retail/residential mix, Kentlands, Md.

Recreation center adjacent to housing, Kentlands, Md.

Elementary school kids can walk to, Kentlands, Md.

Town hall, South Riding, Va.

Corner store, Belmont Forest, Va.

Housing in different price ranges, Wyndecrest, Md.

Hide the Car

Duplex dominated by garages

Duplex with hidden garages

Front yard garage

Garage in rear, South Riding, Va.

More good examples:

Garage with apartment above, Kentlands, Md.

Rear lane with garages, Kentlands, Md.

Provide Parks and Open Space

Typical townhouse complex with no green space

Townhouse complex facing park, Falls Church

More good examples:

Community green, Kentlands, Md.

Community open space, Baldwin Place, Staunton

Community Park, Fincastle, Botetourt County

Village green, Prairie Crossing, Grayslake, Ill.

Use Good Design

Good design is attractive:

New townhouses, Reston

New hotel, Ashland

Good design can ease conflicts:

New office in residential area, Chesterfield County

New shopping center, Cape Cod, Mass.

Good design doesn't have to cost more:

New home in Herndon

Office made from pre-manufactured units, Bath County

Strengthen Downtowns

Do you want the heart and soul of your community to be a downtown or a shopping mall?

ALL TRUE COMMUNITIES, whether small town or big city, have downtowns that every citizen knows and comes to. These hubs often are the clearest expression of a community, the mental image people take with them. Almost written off the economic balance sheet in the 1970s, many downtowns are experiencing revitalization.

What is the "picture" that occurs to you when you think of your community? Is it the mall? Or the downtown?

A downtown serves many functions. Typically the most significant public buildings are located here, such as government offices, the courthouse, the library, or the post office. Stores, apartments, offices, and museums increase the reasons for frequenting the area. Each use reinforces the others.

Downtowns are human scale, meant for people of all ages and walks of life. People come here during the day for business and on evenings and weekends for restaurants, concerts, or parades. This is the place where you "run into" old acquaintances and feel part of a distinct community. Downtowns often include a walking district created before the automobile era.

The successful city of the future will have a vibrant central city, limit bad sprawl and promote smart growth.

William Hudnutt, ULI

Public commitment to downtown encourages private investment. Local government facilities are often the backbone of the downtown, while a well-developed public realm lets people gather informally. It is this complex intermingling of public and private, interior and exterior that cannot be replaced by far-flung shopping malls and separate government offices.

Economic and social vitality in the core has a positive impact on the entire community. Ongoing reinvestment in the core area raises property values and uses infrastructure efficiently. Conversely, the stakes are high, because the alternative is a hollow core. All of the communities in Virginia have distinctive traditional core areas and there are many examples throughout the state of successful and vibrant downtowns.

Tools for Downtown Revitalization:

- Use the Main Street Approach
- Encourage Infill Development
- Provide Incentives for Downtown Housing
- Keep Government Offices Downtown
- Develop Fairs, Festivals and Farmers Markets
- Create an Attractive Streetscape

Use the Main Street Approach

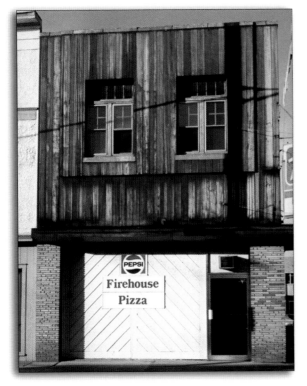

© National Main Street Center

Do your historic downtown buildings look like this? Or like this?

T HE MAIN STREET MODEL is alive and well in Virginia. This highly successful strategy helps preserve not only the heritage of a community's downtown but also its economy. The Virginia Main Street program provides intensive services and technical support to the 16 active, designated Virginia communities, shown on the map here.

Through the Main Street approach, thousands of communities across the nation have revitalized their downtowns. While this approach takes effort and commitment, the results prove that downtowns still have what it takes.

Any community can apply the principles of the Main Street model. In fact, using these time-tested strategies, particularly building broad-based commitment to the downtown, can only add to other initiatives.

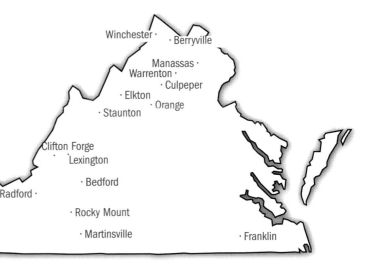

THINGS YOU SHOULD KNOW:

- Between 1985 and December 1999, Virginia's Main Street communities gained 1,700 net new businesses, added 3,725 net new jobs to downtown payrolls, completed 2,793 building improvements, and sparked $108.7 million in private investment.

The Main Street Program Is a Four-Point Approach:

■ Design

Enhancing the unique visual quality of downtown by addressing all design elements to create an appealing environment. First impressions count. Decades of neglect and misguided improvement have taken a toll on the appearance of many downtowns and their economic potential. Renovated facades, creative merchandising displays, appropriate landscaping, and public improvements are all part of downtown's long-lasting visual appeal and a well functioning physical environment.

■ Promotion

Creating and marketing a positive image based on the unique attributes of the downtown district. After decades of neglect, visitors and investors may perceive downtown as dead, with little chance of recovery. Using a comprehensive promotions calendar with special events, retail promotions, and on-going public relations, downtown can reverse old perceptions.

■ Economic Restructuring

Strengthening downtown's existing economic assets and fulfilling its broadest market potential. The retail environment has changed profoundly. To become competitive, the downtown district must reposition itself. With a thorough understanding of today's market, downtown can develop strategies to enhance the competitiveness of existing merchants, recruit new businesses, create new anchors, and convert tired space into new uses.

■ Organization

Establishing consensus and cooperation by building effective partnerships among all downtown stakeholders. The downtown constituency is unique and not always well served by traditional economic and business development groups. An on-going management and advocacy organization dedicated to downtown fosters revitalization progress and sustainability.

Adapted from *Building Economic Vitality Downtown*, 1998 Annual Report, Virginia Main Street Program.

■ Designated Main Street communities receive services directed at individual community needs. Façade designs for individual buildings are one such service. Staunton used the program to develop a comprehensive streetscape plan, which has been implemented.

■ Any community or organization interested in downtown redevelopment has ready access to the Virginia Main Street library and resource materials, as well as limited on-site assistance from Main Street staff.

■ Since 1985, Lexington has seen 151 building renovations with a total private investment of nearly $8 million.

■ Tourism to downtown Manassas increased 120% from 1997 to 1998, in large part due to the Manassas Railway Festival coordinated by Historic Manassas, Inc.

■ Since the establishment of the Cyberstreet Technology Zone in downtown Winchester in late 1997, more than 94 new jobs have been created, and property improvements as a result of business investment total $2.3 million.

Rehabbed bank, downtown Elkton

FOR MORE INFORMATION:

Designing the Successful Downtown, Urban Land Institute, Washington, DC, 1988; (202) 624-7000.

The Main Street Movie (video), National Main Street Center; (202) 588-6219.

Main Street Success Stories, National Main Street Center; (202) 588-6219.

Revitalizing Downtown, National Main Street Center; (202) 588-6219.

National Main Street Center, 1785 Massachusetts Ave., N.W., Washington, DC 20036; (202) 588-6219.

Virginia Downtown Development Association, P.O. Box 12152, Falls Church, VA 22042; (703) 538-7079.

Virginia Main Street Program, 501 North Second Street, Richmond, VA 23219; (804) 371-7030.

Build Livable Communities

Virginia Main Street Program - Cumulative Statistics
1985 – 1999

Community	Net New Businesses	Net New Jobs	Volunteer Investment[+]	Rehabs Completed	Private Investment
Bedford	97	209	1,478	337	$6,867,210
Berryville	34	78	1,295	127	$3,557,008
Clifton Forge	22	46	1,570.75	16	$2,368,111
Culpeper	131	193.5	3,010	237	$6,159,588
Elkton	30	61	3,024.75	35	$1,517,281
Franklin*	117	327	1,223	286	$9,530,514
Lexington	102	195	3,083	151	$7,925,923
Manassas	66	197	3,641.75	61	$5,526,355
Marion	33	53	5,153	24	$316,050
Martinsville	36	193.5	1,915	25	$1,208,068
Orange	81	223.5	5,811	192	$6,297,658
Radford	47	233	3,092	106	$4,261,201
Rocky Mount	11	35.5	3,578	44	$981,556
Staunton	37	137	2,695	76	$4,167,812
Warrenton	96	163	8,364	261	$10,318,959
Winchester	191	626	5,141	147	$19,329,243
Inactive Programs	576	796	2,000	687	$18,883,719
TOTAL	1,707	3,767	55,985.25	2,812	$109,216,256

* Community statistics are incomplete for 1999 due to flooding from Hurricane Floyd
[+] Volunteer investment shows 1997-99 figures only.

Source: Virginia Main Street Program Monthly Reports

Create an Inviting Streetscape

STREETSCAPE CONSISTS OF street paving, sidewalks, streetlights, traffic lights, public signs, street "furniture" such as benches and trash cans, landscaping, and public art. In downtowns and neighborhood commercial areas, a pleasing streetscape can repay its cost in increased tourism and shopping revenue, increased citizen use of public spaces, enhanced civic pride, and new investment by the private sector. The most effective streetscapes are a rich mosaic of individual elements that create interest and provide comfort for pedestrians and reflect the historic character of the area. The interplay between public and private efforts reinforces the vitality of the streetscape.

Communities should consider putting utilities underground or moving them to the rear of buildings.

Staunton downtown before...

...and after utilities were placed underground

Williamsburg and Front Royal have undergrounded utilities on their main commercial strips leading into downtown. Lexington long ago placed the utilities underground in its downtown district, and Staunton has done the same. These communities recognize that overhead poles and wires are a major distraction to the beauty of their historic commercial cores.

THINGS YOU SHOULD KNOW:

- Waterford received a Transportation Enhancement grant from VDOT to underground utility wires and manage traffic in the historic village.

- Staunton's "Big Dig" was more than the standard upgrade of water and sewer lines. Brick sidewalks with granite curbs and historically styled traffic lights, street lights, and street signs were installed. Utilities, including electrical, gas, telephone, cable, and fiber optics, were placed underground.

- Downtown Lexington has been used for movie sets, including the Civil War drama *Sommersby*, because of its combination of historic buildings and lack of overhead wires.

FOR MORE INFORMATION:

Public Improvements Program (slide show and monograph), National Main Street Center, Washington, DC, (202) 588-6219, or borrow from the Virginia Main Street Program, (804) 371-7030.

Streetscape Improvements

Underground utilities, Charlottesville

Outdoor dining, Winchester

© WINCHESTER OLD TOWN DEVELOPMENT BOARD

Public art, Falls Church

Farmers Market, Staunton

New public park, Ballston

Canal Walk, Richmond

Streetscape improvements, Staunton

Reshape the Strip

Which is better for the community? Abandoning older buildings every time a new store comes in?
Or rejuvenating existing shopping centers like the one on the right?

PEOPLE LIKE THE CONVENIENCE and low prices of discount stores, supermarkets, and chain restaurants, but the same people often complain about the ugliness and traffic congestion associated with commercial strip development. Progress does not require turning every major road corridor into an endless parade of parking lots, pole signs, and bland strip shopping centers. Commercial strips can be redesigned to make them more attractive, less congested, and more convenient for shoppers and pedestrians.

What Are the Characteristics of the Strip?
- A reliance on cars to go everywhere
- Traffic congestion
- Lots of big signs, traffic lights, and driveways
- Streetscape dominated by asphalt parking lots
- Little or no landscaping
- Cheap looking, boxy architecture
- Every town starts to look alike

Communities all over Virginia are starting to reshape the strip, and savvy developers are leading the way. New walkable town centers are becoming more common throughout the Commonwealth. Communities are placing limits on the length of commercial districts, pole signs are being replaced with monument signs, street trees and landscaped parking lots are being

required in more locations, and cluttered strips are even being turned into attractive boulevards.

Seven Steps to Reshaping the Strip
Communities can begin the process of reclaiming existing commercial strips by agreeing to a long-term design program that gradually transforms strips into mixed-use town centers. These steps can help:

1. **Put a firm limit on the length of any commercial district;** instead of a longer strip, allow commercial expansion in greater depth. This concentrates commercial uses and encourages shared parking and walking between stores.

2. **Limit curb cuts and consolidate entrances** along the road to a few main driveways with internal service streets based on a block system to connect businesses. This relieves traffic back-ups, accidents, and the need for expensive road widening.

3. **Help unify the streetscape with continuous street trees,** high-quality parking-lot landscaping and, where possible, planted medians in the main roadway to prevent unlimited left-hand turns.

4. **Build sidewalks and crosswalks** throughout the

area to encourage shared parking, public transportation, and walking between stores and to nearby homes and offices.

5. **Build a street frontage** by filling in the front of large parking lots with small, closely spaced storefronts with parking behind or on the side.

6. **Provide incentives** for the use of attractive, place-responsive architecture, smaller signs, and multistory buildings.

7. **Encourage a mix of other uses,** including nearby housing, to begin to build a walkable neighborhood rather than a driving-only strip district.

THINGS YOU SHOULD KNOW:

- A national survey found that 86% of consumers would prefer to shop in a town center with a mix of stores and civic buildings rather than a strip shopping center.

- There are more than 20 town center developments completed or under construction in the greater Washington, D.C., area.

- Reston Town Center in Fairfax County is a walkable, mixed-use development that includes housing, offices, movie theaters, an ice-skating rink, and a wide array of national chains and locally owned stores.

Sycamore Square Shopping Center, Chesterfield County

- In Mashpee, Massachusetts, an old strip shopping center was reoriented so that buildings face onto a new "Main Street." A greater concentration of businesses was possible and the project has been highly successful.

- Owners of Willow Oak Plaza in Waynesboro (pictured on page 58) overhauled the 1960s-era shopping center with extensive landscaping, coordinated signs, and an attractive color scheme. The response: a significant increase in business. Contact Malcolm Jones, (540) 942-5101.

- A number of communities use design guidelines to control the look of development along major corridors. Among them are Chesterfield County, which sets a design theme for specific areas and requires all buildings to be compatible with this theme. Fort Collins, Colorado, has detailed design guidelines specifically for retail centers.

- Charlottesville, Leesburg, Lexington, Williamsburg, and Albemarle County require design review for projects on major highway corridors leading into historic districts.

- Communities also restrict where development can go, in order to maintain clear corridors and concentrate retail activity. Cary, North Carolina, for example, requires retail/commercial uses to locate in established activity centers. Some localities set a minimum distance between such nodes of activity.

- Lexington's Nelson Street corridor, formerly a typical commercial strip, is gradually being restyled into an attractive gateway to this historic city. In addition to public streetscape improvements, the city is encouraging private site improvements. The city provides architectural design assistance and even pays for landscaping and smaller sign posts for willing property owners. Contact Planning Director, City of Lexington, (540) 463-7134.

Alternatives to the Strip

Typical Barnes & Noble, set within a sea of asphalt.

Barnes & Noble in downtown Bethesda, Md., is built right up to the sidewalk.

Shopping center in Chesterfield County hides the parking.

Cascades Village Center in Loudoun County creates a new downtown.

Creekside in Frederick County features attractive new buildings.

FOR MORE INFORMATION:

Designing Urban Corridors, PAS Report #418, by Kirk R. Bishop, 1990, American Planning Association Planners Book Service, Chicago, IL; (312) 786-6344.

Shared Parking, Urban Land Institute, Washington, D.C., 1987; (202) 624-7000.

Shopping Center Development Handbook, 3rd Edition, Urban Land Institute, Washington, D.C., 1999; (202) 624-7000.

What Developers Can Do to Alleviate Public Opposition to Development

1. **Support open space protection efforts** - The loss of natural areas and green spaces is one of the major reasons for growing anti-development sentiment. Open space plans give citizens the assurance that special places will be preserved and make it less likely they will fight development everywhere.

2. **Save the trees** - Few things upset people more than cutting down large trees. Studies show consumers prefer, and will pay more for, homes with trees. Mature trees that are preserved during development add more value to a lot than post-construction landscaping.

3. **Stop building look-alike houses** - Many consumers are turned off by cookie-cutter subdivisions and the homogeneous look of new tract houses. Visual preference surveys show that citizens prefer designs that reflect vernacular architecture, are compatible with their surroundings, and are located within traditional style neighborhoods.

4. **Hide the garages** - The most prominent feature of most new houses is a gaping front-yard garage. More popular, traditionally styled houses hide garages in the rear, on the side, or in a lane at the back of the property.

5. **Provide public plazas and places to walk** - Walking is the single most popular form of outdoor recreation in America. Yet new suburbs provide few places to walk and almost no place to mingle except the mall. Consumers rank walking and bicycle paths as one of the top features they desire in new communities.

6. **Build town centers, not strip centers** - People like convenient parking, but more than 80 percent of consumers say they "like the idea of an old fashioned Southern or New England town" with small shops and green space. Two-thirds say small stores in a town center are likely to offer "better service as well as opportunities for socializing with your neighbors."

7. **Recognize that design is more important than density** - Attractive, well planned, cluster developments can be more profitable than conventional subdivisions, especially in rural areas. On the other hand, well planned, compact village development fits better with historic town or neighborhood character than low-density sprawl.

8. **Cooperate with environmentalists for mutual benefit** - Developers and environmentalists actually have much in common. What's good for business can also be good for the environment and the community as a whole. Relaxing residential street standards, allowing natural stormwater systems, reducing the size of parking lots, and other measures can reduce the costs of development while improving environmental protection.

FOR MORE INFORMATION:

Best Development Practices: Doing the Right Thing and Making Money at the Same Time, by Reid Ewing, American Planning Association; (312) 786-6344.

Trends and Innovations in Master Planned Communities, by Urban Land Institute, 1998; (800) 321-5011.

Know the Value of History

Do you think more tourists visit George Washington's home at Mt. Vernon, or the site of his boyhood home in Stafford County?

THE HUMAN FORCES that have shaped Virginia for nearly 400 years are evident today in the many historic buildings and sites that dot the state's landscape. Native American burial sites, historic farmhouses, Civil War battlefields, old mills, stone barns and unique agricultural structures, rural hamlets and villages, river plantations, spring resorts, quaint downtowns and pre-World War II neighborhoods, even older roads and bridges tell distinct stories about each region of the state.

Virginia's Tidewater is the site of Jamestown—the nation's first permanent English settlement, and colonial history is evident throughout the region. Williamsburg, the 18th century colonial capital, the James River plantations, and numerous villages and hamlets dating from the 17th and 18th century tell the story of the early settlers turning the land to commerce and establishing government.

> *The man who feels no sentiment or veneration for the memory of his forefathers is himself unworthy of kindred regard and remembrance.*
>
> Daniel Webster

The Piedmont, settled in the early 18th century, reflects the establishment of Virginia's agricultural and industrial economy. It was the home to three American presidents—Jefferson, Madison, and Monroe—as well as Chief Justice John Marshall. The Piedmont was a critical battleground during the Civil War and the site of many key engagements, including Chancellorsville, Fredericksburg, The Wilderness, First and Second Manassas, and Brandy Station.

Western Virginia and the Shenandoah Valley were the site of two historical events that are of lasting interest to Americans all over the continent. As the staging ground for westward emigration in the late 1700s and 1800s, the Valley and the ridges and valleys to the west are places to which many Americans trace their ancestors. In the 1860s, the Valley bore the full brunt of the Civil War, the nation's most searing conflict. Its landscape offers tales not only of the fighting but of the daily tribulations on the home front.

Virginia's historic buildings, neighborhoods, and landscapes are tremendous assets to the state. They give us a sense of identity and stability. They physically connect us to the past, while also providing an immense attraction to visitors from throughout the world.

Much of Virginia's heritage is found in small towns and rural areas. Scattered historic buildings and their landscape context make up much of what has always defined our state; whether along the waterways of the Tidewater region, the rolling hills of the Piedmont, or the steep slopes and valleys of the Blue Ridge. However, much of the new development in Virginia is occurring in unincorporated rural areas. This raises the challenge for communities individually and the state as a whole to recognize the value of rural historic sites, to identify the most important features, and to develop ways to retain the historic integrity of these resources.

Virginia's urban heritage is also threatened by the abandonment of historic school buildings, post offices, and other historic structures. Likewise, road construction, insensitive new development and suburban sprawl threaten Virginia's historic resources. As with our natural resources, we must identify what is important and develop strategies to maintain our historic resources.

Historic Preservation Is Good for Business

PRESERVING HISTORIC ASSETS is good for the heart and soul, but it also makes economic sense. In fact, studies in Virginia, Maryland, North Carolina, and other states confirm that preservation projects have a greater economic impact than other projects.

- Tourists spend $9.1 billion in Virginia every year. Historic and cultural sites are the number one attraction in the Commonwealth.

- According to the Travel Industry Association of America, historic preservation visitors stay longer and spend more than other visitors. They stay an average of 4.7 nights per visit compared with 3.3 nights for other travelers; they spend an average of $615 per trip, compared with $425 for other travelers; and they are more likely to stay in a hotel, motel or bed and breakfast inn.

- Every $1 million spent on the rehabilitation of an historic building creates 15.6 construction jobs and 14.2 jobs elsewhere in the economy and adds $779,800 to household incomes.

- Every $1 million spent on historic rehabilitation creates 3.4 more jobs and adds $53,500 more to Virginia household incomes than $1 million in new construction.

- Studies show that historic districts help increase property values for both commercial and residential properties.

- Since creating a preservation revolving fund, Historic Winchester has leveraged $110,000 in working capital into nearly $2.7 million, used to buy, restore, and sell 64 historic buildings.

FOR MORE INFORMATION:

The Economic Benefits of Preservation: Making the Case, by Donovan D. Rypkema, National Trust for Historic Preservation; (202) 588-6000.

Virginia's Economy and Preservation: The Impact of Preservation on Jobs, Business, and Community, Preservation Alliance of Virginia, 1996, Charlottesville, VA; (804) 984-4484.

Identify and Designate Historic Sites

Thomas Wolfe can't go home again; his birthplace is now a parking lot.

THE MANY HISTORIC BUILDINGS AND SITES in Virginia are a testament to the wise stewardship of current and previous owners. But as development increases throughout the state, so does the threat that these resources may be destroyed, often through lack of awareness of their value.

Historic preservation is a three-step process: identify, designate, and protect. The foundation of historic preservation is awareness—identification of historic sites and what makes them important. Architectural surveys have been completed for many localities in Virginia. Others could take this step.

Designation recognizes particularly important historic sites, buildings, or areas. Individual buildings as well as districts can be nominated to the National Register of Historic Places and the Virginia Landmarks Register.

National Register listing informs local, state, and federal governments of the existence of important historic

Preservation brings new jobs, new businesses, good wages, significant tourist traffic, and economic benefit.

Virginia's Economy and Historic Preservation

resources. National Register listing provides a degree of protection against harmful actions of the federal government such as road widenings, construction, or demolition projects. It also provides financial benefits to property owners in the form of federal and state tax credits. On the other hand, National Register listing is purely honorary. It does not regulate or restrict the actions of private owners or localities in any way.

Virginia has 230 National Register Historic Districts. A good number are in cities or towns, but districts can be villages, agricultural complexes, other related clusters of buildings, or broad landscapes. Virginia has 12 Rural Historic Districts, the largest of which are the Madison-Barbour Historic District and Southwest Mountains Historic District in Orange and Albemarle counties. Together these two districts total 63,175 acres. Many more places in Virginia could qualify as historic districts, particularly small towns and villages.

There are two primary avenues for protecting historic properties. First, property owners who want to permanently protect a site's historic features can use an historic easement. Second, communities that want to protect historic resources can enact a local historic district ordinance. This is a good way to ensure that new development is compatible with historic buildings and sites. Typically these ordinances guard against unnecessary demolitions and insensitive new development or alterations to the exterior of buildings. Making sure that these historic places remain also helps to protect investment and increase tourism.

THINGS YOU SHOULD KNOW:

- In Virginia, more than 1,900 historic resources are listed on the National Register. Properties in historic districts bring this number to more than 35,000.

Urban National Register historic district, Richmond

Rural National Register historic district, Clarke County

- Approximately 60 localities in Virginia have local historic district ordinances, including Alexandria, Middleburg, Norfolk, Richmond, Roanoke, Smithfield and other communities large and small.

Historic easement: Waverley House, Staunton

- Studies show that property values increase more in historic areas than non-historic areas. For example, between 1987 and 1995, residential properties in Staunton's five historic districts appreciated from 51.9 to 66.0 percent, compared to 51.1% or less for properties outside of historic districts. Commercial gains were even more dramatic—a 27.7 to 256.4% increase for properties in historic districts versus an average of 25.2% for commercial properties outside historic districts.

- Many historic neighborhoods also offer modest-priced housing, with the opportunity for substantial appreciation of property values.

- Historic easements protect 265 properties in Virginia. Historic easements in Virginia protect sites ranging from historic farmhouses to city residences to Civil War battlefields.

- Green Springs in Louisa County was the first Rural Historic District to be designated a National Historic Landmark district in Virginia.

© Preservation Alliance of Virginia

- Rural Historic District designation can help protect communities against ill-advised highway "improvement" projects and can be a catalyst for stronger protective measures such as zoning and easements.

Buffalo Springs herb farm, Rockbridge County

- Virginia communities can enact design standards for new construction on highway corridors leading into historic districts.

FOR MORE INFORMATION:

Guiding Growth in Virginia: Local Incentives for Revitalization & Preservation, Environmental Law Institute, November 1998. Call (202) 939-3800 or contact law@eli.org.

Preparing a Historic Preservation Plan, PAS Report #450, American Planning Association; (312) 786-6344.

Virginia's Rural Historic Districts: Making the Case, Preservation Alliance of Virginia, 1998; (804) 984-4484.

Find New Uses for Old Buildings

Pampered Palate, Staunton, before and after: Which do you think attracts more customers?

VIRGINIANS SHARE A HERITAGE that is among the oldest and richest in America. This heritage is as diverse as the colonial capital of Williamsburg, the historic market in Roanoke, Monument Avenue in Richmond, the waterfront of Alexandria, the homes of Presidents and patriots, battlefields from the Revolutionary and Civil Wars, and the historic villages and towns all across the Commonwealth.

Statewide, 1,900 buildings, districts and sites are listed on the National Register of Historic Places. These historic buildings, neighborhoods and sites give Virginia its unique sense of place. Historic buildings are important because they physically connect us to the past. They tell us who we are and where we came from.

Saving historic buildings is also important because it makes economic sense. Preservation brings new jobs and businesses. It attracts tourists and retirees and it enhances property values and quality of life.

THINGS YOU SHOULD KNOW:

- Historic preservation is a big business in Virginia. Preservation brings new jobs, new and expanded businesses, good wages, significant tourist expenditures and economic benefits to all Virginians.

- Nearly 75% of first-time visitors and over a third of all visitors to Virginia visit historic sites. What's more, historic preservation visitors stay longer, visit twice as many places and spend an average of over two and a half times more money in Virginia than other visitors.

- In Virginia, there are 275 historic attractions which generate over 6.5 million visitors annually. Another 22 million annual visits are made to national park sites including Civil War Battlefields.

- The economic impact of Colonial Williamsburg alone is over half a billion dollars a year to Virginia's economy. Old Town Alexandria generates $8 million dollars a year in lodging and restaurant taxes by visitors drawn to this historic community.

- Property values of historic buildings and sites throughout Virginia almost always go up when buildings are designated for their historic value. This is because scarcity and certainty create value in real estate. Historic resources are a scarce resource and investors, home buyers, and business people are attracted to communities that care enough about these resources to protect them.

- For example, during the 1980s and 1990s, property values in the historic districts in Staunton, Fredericksburg and Richmond grew considerably faster than property values in non-historic areas of these communities.

- In a recent 15-year period, the rehabilitation of some 900 historic buildings throughout Virginia provided 12,697 jobs, about half in the construction trades, and the other half in other fields.

- The rehabilitation of historic structures is generally cost competitive with new construction, but it is much more labor intensive. The net effect of this difference is that the local economic impact of construction expenditures on older buildings is greater than on new buildings.

- Historic rehabilitation has been responsible for restoring economic health to many well-known Virginia landmarks such as the Jefferson Hotel in Richmond, the Homestead in Bath County and the Hotel Roanoke. Less well-known but equally important local landmarks such as the Torpedo Factory in Alexandria, the Tobacco Row Apartments in Richmond, Old Petersburg High School, the Danville Railway Depot, the Smithfield Inn, and dozens of other buildings have provided economic boosts to communities throughout the Commonwealth.

Calhoun's, Harrisonburg, formerly a Woolworth's

Hampton Inn, Lexington, incorporating historic house

Glasgow School, converted to housing for the elderly

Alleghany Building, Clifton Forge, rehabilitated for affordable housing

The economic benefits of historic preservation are enormous. The knowledge of the economic benefits of preservation is minuscule.

Don Rypkema,
Economics of Historic Preservation

Former downtown Leggett's Department Store, now Staunton City Hall

F & M Bank, Bridgewater

Lyric condos, Lexington

FOR MORE INFORMATION:

Economics of Historic Buildings: A Community Leader's Guide, by Donovan D. Rypkema, National Trust for Historic Preservation, Washington, DC, 1994; (202) 588-6000.

New Uses for Obsolete Buildings, by Urban Land Institute, Washington, DC, 1996; (202)–624-7000.

Virginia's Economy and Historic Preservation, by Preservation Alliance of Virginia, Charlottesville, VA, 1996; (804) 984-4484.

Preserve Battlefields

Doesn't it make sense to preserve Virginia's Civil War battlefields?

VIRGINIA WAS THE SITE for both Revolutionary and Cvil War battles. At Yorktown, British forces surrendered to American and French troops to end the Revolutionary War in 1781. Virginia was also a key state in the Civil War, and the battlegrounds of the Civil War define the character of many Virginia communities. But the lands where armies clashed, where bravery and sacrifice turned farm fields into hallowed ground, are today threatened by haphazard development.

A battlefield—whether protected and open to visitors or preserved by a private owner as open space—can be a significant component of a community's well-being, yielding economic, cultural, and environmental benefits.

Virginia was the location of numerous Civil War strategic campaigns and battles: First and Second Manassas, Fredericksburg, Chancellorsville, Richmond, the Wilderness, and Petersburg, for example. The Shenan-

> *The public cannot expect agricultural land uses to continue to preserve open land that conveniently coincides with Civil War Battlefields.*
>
> Study of Civil War Sites in the Shenandoah Valley, National Park Service, 1992.

doah Valley was the site of two strategically important campaigns involving 15 major battles and hundreds of smaller encounters. The Civil War ended with Lee's surrender at Appomattox.

Several important battlefields in Virginia are protected, at least in part, by the National Park Service, but even many of these are threatened by nearby development. Other Virginia battlefields are located primarily on private land and are even more jeopardized with the threat of future development.

Battlefields Make Dollars and Sense:

- Many Virginia communities are located near historic battlefields, which provide important economic benefits. A battlefield can be a basic industry that generates jobs in a community.

- Battlefields can generate income from tourist expenditures and sales tax revenue. A quarter of all Virginia visitors stop at Civil War sites. Civil War tourists are among the highest daily spenders of all visitors.

- In 1994 tourists at Gettysburg National Military Park generated $100.4 million in expenditures and $6.5 million in state and local tax revenues.

- Battlefields bring additional income into communities through the multiplier effect. Every dollar a visitor spends is multiplied—spent again in the community—an average of two times. For example, at Pea Ridge, Arkansas, the $10.8 million spent by visitors in 1991 had a total economic impact of $20.2 million.

- As historic open space, a battlefield also adds economic value to adjacent properties and enhances a community's quality of life by protecting its natural resources, environmental qualities, and visual amenities.

THINGS YOU SHOULD KNOW:

- Many techniques have been used to protect battlefields. These include land purchases by federal, state, or local government, the use of conservation easements, and the protection of battlefields by nonprofit organizations or private landowners.

- Forty percent of the most threatened Civil War battlefields identified in 1993 by the Civil War Sites Advisory Commission are in Virginia.

- Chancellorsville Battlefield in Spotsylvania County, one of the fastest-growing localities in Virginia, is on the National Trust for Historic Preservation's 1998 list of "America's Most Endangered Historic Places."

Piedmont Battlefield, part of Middle River agricultural district, Augusta County

McDowell Battlefield, Highland County

© PATRICIA LANZA

Salem Church, Chancellorsville Battlefield, Spotsylvania County

- The Shenandoah Valley Battlefields National Historic District Commission has been formed by Congress to devise a plan to protect and interpret ten Civil War sites in the Valley.

- Frederick County recognizes the importance of the county's Civil War sites in its comprehensive plan.

- Piedmont Battlefield in Augusta County is part of an approximately 9,000-acre agricultural district.

- Spotsylvania County has developed voluntary design guidelines for new development on lands adjacent to National Park Service battlefield properties.

- Virginia's Civil War Trails recognizes, organizes, and interprets 250 Civil War sites throughout the state.

- Lee's Retreat, a popular and effective multi-jurisdictional marketing effort in Southside, Virginia, ties together sites touched by the Confederate Army under General Robert E. Lee during the last days of the Civil War.

- In 2000, the Virginia General Assembly approved $3.4 million in state funding for Civil War battlefield protection.

FOR MORE INFORMATION:

"Battlefield Network Plan," Frederick County Department of Planning and Development, February 1997; (540) 665-5651.

Civil War Heritage Preservation: A Study of Alternatives, by Elizabeth B. Waters. Available from American Battlefield Protection Program, National Park Service, 1849 C Street, N.W., Washington, DC 20240; (202) 343-3449.

Civil War Preservation Trust, 1515 Wilson Boulevard, Suite 350, Arlington, VA 22209; (703) 682-2350.

Dollar$ and Sense of Battlefield Preservation: A Handbook for Community Leaders, Frances H. Kennedy and Douglas R. Porter, National Trust for Historic Preservation, Preservation Books, 1999; (202) 588-6296.

Choices for Virginia Communities

 **Chain Drug Stores**

 **Fast Food Restaurants**

 **Gas Station Canopies**

 **Ice Cream Parlors**

Choices for Virginia Communities

Franchise Signs

Cellular Towers

Motorist Information

Big Box Retailers

Choices for Virginia Communities

Public Buildings

Battlefield Preservation

Strip Development

Main Street Retail

Choices for Virginia Communities

Transit-Oriented Development

Scenic Highways

Transportation Solutions

Highway Bridges

Set the Standard with Public Buildings

Which of these new public buildings better expresses the dignity, permanence and importance of civic institutions?

PEOPLE HAVE LONG UNDERSTOOD that public buildings can help nurture feelings of heritage and community that enrich a nation and its people. Public buildings and spaces create identity and sense of place. They give communities something to remember and admire. The challenge facing public architecture is to provide every generation with structures that link them with their past, fill them with pride, and reinforce their sense of belonging.

Public buildings should set the standard in a community. Public buildings with civic stature, quality materials, and prominent settings project a sense of permanence and human scale that expresses the dignity and importance of public institutions.

During the 18th, 19th, and first half of the 20th centuries, public buildings in Virginia such as city halls, courthouses, post offices, and public schools were always the community's most beautiful and important buildings. In the last half of the 20th century, however, public buildings often have been relegated to little

more than utilitarian boxes. We sometimes have designed schools and libraries that resemble correctional facilities. We have built fire stations and post offices that look like warehouses, and we have moved many of our public buildings from downtown to new locations on the strip outside of town.

People appreciate public buildings that express the dignity, permanence, and importance of civic institutions and which harmonize with their surroundings. There are a number of instances in Virginia where communities have demanded higher quality in the design of new public buildings and resisted efforts to move post offices, city halls, and other civic institutions to out-of-the-way locations.

The buildings above—the Town Hall in Bridgewater and the offices of the Virginia Department of Environmental Quality in the Shenandoah Valley—reflect two very different approaches to new public architecture in Virginia. On the next page are examples of handsome public buildings in Virginia and elsewhere.

Public Buildings with Civic Stature

Judicial Center, Harrisonburg

City Hall, Leesburg

City Hall, Herndon

Fire station, Luray

*Public buildings in
size, form and elegance
must look beyond
the present day.*

George Washington

Woodstock School, Shenandoah County, rehabilitated
for county offices

Post Offices

Typical small-town post office

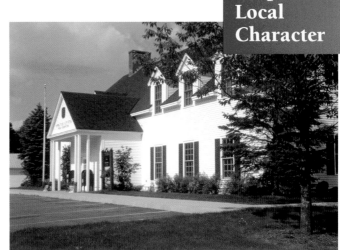

Stowe, Vt., post office

Leesburg post office

Rockbridge Baths post office

FOR MORE INFORMATION:

Design Review, PAS Report #454, American Planning Association, 1995; (312) 786-6344.

Designing the City: A Guide for Advocates and Public Officials, by Adele Fleet Bacow, Island Press, 1995; (800) 828-1302.

"Keeping the Post Office Downtown," by Kenneth Smith and Laura Skaggs, *Forum News,* National Trust for Historic Preservation, July/August, 1997; (202) 588-6000.

The mayor is the chief architect of the city, who must understand how public design policies can influence, for better or worse, the urban built environment.

Joe Riley, Mayor of Charleston, S.C.

Ask Franchises and Chain Stores To Fit In

Which of these fast food franchises made an attempt to fit in with the local community?

DO FRANCHISES AND CHAIN STORES in Virginia have to be in the same style building as those in New York, North Carolina, or Nevada? The answer is "of course not."

National franchises and chain stores can and do change their standard building design to "fit in" with the local character of the surrounding community. But they only do this in communities savvy enough to insist on something better than "off-the-shelf," cookie-cutter architecture.

Experience shows that if you accept standard look-alike corporate design, this is what you'll get. On the other hand, if your community insists on a customized, site-specific design, that is what you will get. To understand how, see the tips on pages 80 and 81.

The bottom line for most chain stores and franchises is securing access to profitable trade areas. They evaluate locations based on their economic potential. If they are asked to address local historic preservation, site planning, or architectural concerns, they will usually do so.

Fast-food restaurants, gas stations, convenience stores, and chain drug stores are some of the most prominent

> *We shape our buildings and afterwards, our buildings shape us.*
>
> Winston Churchill

buildings in our auto-oriented society, and their look-alike architecture contributes to the homogenization of Virginia communities. Chain drugstores, for example, are proliferating across the state. Dozens of large, single-story featureless buildings are being constructed on downtown corners—often after historic buildings have been razed. Likewise, massive "big box" retailers have overwhelmed many smaller communities, physically as well as economically. But as more communities have recognized the economic value of preserving their sense of place, there increasingly are examples of where these huge companies have adapted their designs or even their locations to meet local standards.

Today, communities all across America, including many in Virginia, are working successfully with franchises and chain stores to get buildings that fit in. See the examples that follow.

THINGS YOU SHOULD KNOW:

■ Design review is one means of ensuring the compatibility of franchise design with local community character.

- More than 3,000 cities, towns, and counties nationwide exercise some type of design review, including close to 60 in Virginia.

- Chesterfield County has done a particularly outstanding job of using design standards to get fast-food restaurants and chain stores to respect local community character. Contact the Chesterfield County Planning Department, P.O. Box 40, Chesterfield, VA 23832; (804) 748-1050; planning@ chesterfield.va.us.

- Even without a design review ordinance, a community can develop voluntary design guidelines. These can help to foster new buildings in harmony with their surroundings, especially if combined with public education and incentives.

- Most fast-food restaurants in Europe are in restored historic buildings.

- The Taco Bell in Fort Collins, Colorado, is in a restored Spanish Colonial Revival house. It has won two awards and is among the top-grossing restaurants in their system.

Award-winning Taco Bell, Ft. Collins, Colo.

- Fast-food restaurants that respect community character can be found in Alexandria, Arlington, Albemarle County, Charlottesville, Falls Church, Fairfax County, James City County, Leesburg, Loudoun County, Reston, Richmond, Rockbridge County, Williamsburg, and other Virginia communities.

- Many communities, including Fauquier County and Warrenton, Virginia, have placed limits on the size of retail stores.

- Other communities limit the amount of land covered by the building, in effect allowing more square footage in additional stories. Gaithersburg, Maryland, for example, limits commercial buildings to 60,000 square feet per floor, thus encouraging multi-story buildings.

- "Big boxes" have located in downtowns or in existing buildings. Toys-R-Us has two-story downtown buildings in several communities, including Santa Monica, California. Wal-Mart has located in a recycled Woolworth's building in Bennington, Vermont, and in a vacant Kmart in downtown Rutland, Vermont.

FOR MORE INFORMATION:

Better Models for Chain Drugstores, by Anne Stillman, Preservation Information Series, National Trust for Historic Preservation, 1999; (202) 588-6000.

Better Models for Superstores: Alternatives to Big-Box Sprawl, by Constance E. Beaumont, Preservation Information Series, National Trust for Historic Preservation, 1997; (202) 588-6000.

"Quarter Pounders with History: Fast Food Outlets Get a Face Lift," by Edward T. McMahon, *Planners Casebook,* American Planning Association, Summer 1996; available from The Conservation Fund, (703) 525-6300.

Saving Face: How Corporate Franchise Design Can Respect Community Identity, PAS Report 452, by Ronald Lee Fleming, American Planning Association; (312) 786-6344.

"Shaping the Design of Chesterfield County," Chesterfield County Planning Department, (804) 748-1050. This brochure explains the county's overall design philosophy. The county also has a Design Standards Manual that describes the county's standards for landscaping, signs, and architectural compatibility.

Fast-Food Restaurants that Fit In

McDonald's, Richmond

McDonald's, Freeport, Me.

Burger King, Richmond

Burger King, Chesterfield

McDonald's, Alexandria

Burger King, Key West, Fla.

McDonald's, St. Louis, Mo.

Gas Stations and Convenience Stores

Typical service station

New service station, Vt.

Typical convenience store

New convenience store, Charlottesville

More good examples:

Texaco station, Hanover County

Amoco station, City of Bedford

Chain Drugstores

Typical chain drugstore

New Rite Aid, Camden, Me.

New CVS, Alexandria

Lessons Learned

- **Ask, and you may receive.** Experience shows that if you accept the standard "cookie-cutter" design, that's what you'll get. On the other hand, if your community insists on a customized, place-responsive building, then that is what you'll get. The bottom line for most chain stores is securing access to good trade areas. They evaluate locations based on their economic potential. If they are required to address local site planning or architectural concerns, they will usually do so. Hundreds of local communities have successfully worked with national chains and franchises to get buildings that respect local community identity. Your community can too.

- **Use incentives and public opinion, too.** In cases where chain stores and franchises insist on placing corporate interest over community interest, local government can use a variety of regulations and incentives to foster compatibility between franchises and communities. These include incentives, such as relaxed parking standards, density bonuses, and tax credits, as well as regulatory techniques such as historic districts, design guidelines and review, conditional use permits, site plan review, corridor overlay zones, sign controls, and landscape ordinances. However, with or without legal tools, no community should forget the power of public opinion. Many of the successes featured here grew out of public calls for a site-specific design or for saving a cherished building.

- **Reconsider the location of the playground.** Fast-food chains sometimes insist on building a large playground in front of their building. If this is inappropriate for your site, stand firm. There are thousands of highly profitable fast-food restaurants without gaudy outdoor playgrounds. And, there are alternatives. In Charlottesville, Virginia,

Kmart, Jackson, Wyo.

for example, the new Colonial-style McDonald's includes an indoor playground available to children all seasons of the year, good weather or bad.

■ **Drive-thrus provide leverage.** Americans love to drive, so it is no surprise that businesses offering drive-thru facilities are so popular. However, given the pedestrian orientation of most downtowns and neighborhood commercial areas, drive-thru windows can present both urban design and safety problems. First, recognize that drive-thrus are not a requirement. There are many profitable drug stores and fast-food eateries without drive-thrus. However, national chains often argue that drive-thrus are a necessity even in pedestrian-oriented locations. In fact, without a drive-thru the total number of customers may be identical, but the point of sale will be different. Making drive-thrus conditional on design concessions is a very effective technique.

■ **Scrutinize the signs.** Garish, oversized signs are one of the more objectionable aspects of franchises and chains. Left unchecked, the "copy-cat" logic of corporate competition often results in an unsightly clutter of portable signs, pole signs, plastic pennants, flapping flags, and twirling streamers all shouting for attention. Experience shows that sign clutter is ugly, costly, and ineffective. Experience also shows that when signs are controlled, franchis-

es do a better job of selling at less cost, because shoppers can now find what they are looking for. When it comes to signage, businesses want a level playing field. They can compete for attention with 100-foot-tall signs or 10-foot-tall signs. Either way, the burgers taste the same.

■ **The keys to success.** National corporations and their local franchises are more likely to agree to design modifications when:

• Design objectives are clearly stated. The developer and architects should know in advance what criteria will be applied to the proposed project.
• The local government offers pre-application meetings. Misunderstandings can be avoided if the national company is given a chance to meet informally with staff and commission members prior to submitting a formal application.
• Visual design guidelines are available. Many communities no longer rely solely on written design standards. They have adopted visual design guides that graphically depict what constitutes a compatible design.
• Local groups know when to compromise. Fast-food companies care a lot more about some things than others. For example, they are much more adamant about having a drive-thru than they are about architectural styles or sign heights.
• There is organized community support for historic preservation or urban design standards.

Landscape Commercial Areas

Would you prefer to shop at a shopping center heavily landscaped with trees and bushes?
Or at one with no trees and landscaping?

THERE IS NO DOUBT that trees add economic value to residential areas, but what about commercial or institutional property? Here, too, trees and landscaping make dollars and sense. All over the country, in survey after survey, people say they prefer commercial areas with trees and landscaping.

In 1995, the Urban Land Institute conducted a study to determine the impact of trees and landscaping on the value of retail, office, and residential developments. This study found that landscaping and preservation of mature trees "positively affect value for the developers, the users, and the community in many ways." Specifically, the study found that

> *The passage of our Green Law nearly ten years ago has changed the character of this town. At first it was unpopular with developers but later each party claimed it was a good idea.*
>
> Bob Holton, Town of Bridgewater

trees and landscaping have these effects:

• Translate into increased financial returns of 5 to 15% for project developers
• Give developers a competitive edge and increase the rate of project absorption
• Help developers win support for proposed projects, especially in contentious situations
• Establish an image, identity, and sense of community for development projects
• Influence decisions to buy or rent in both residential and commercial projects
• Contribute substantially to the market's perception of security, privacy, and sense of place
• Reduce the need for publicly funded improvements on site and off site
• Contribute to employee productivity, morale, and job satisfaction
• By example, cause other developers to adopt a higher standard of design.

THINGS YOU SHOULD KNOW:

■ More than 50 Virginia communities have landscaping ordinances, including Charlottesville, Falls

Landscaping, Town of Bridgewater

Church, Herndon, Staunton, Virginia Beach, Winchester, and Waynesboro.

- Trees can reduce urban runoff by 17%, decreasing stormwater management costs.

- In a survey of real estate appraisers, 95% of respondents felt that landscaping added to the dollar value of real estate.

- Views of trees and landscape plantings can reduce hospital convalescent stays by up to 8%.

- Forestland produces about 50 tons of sediment per square mile per year. Land stripped for construction produces between 25,000 and 50,000 tons of sediment.

- A one-acre parking lot generates 16 times more polluted runoff than a one-acre meadow.

- 30% of water pollution is generated from parking lot runoff.

- Up to 25% of commercial development costs can be spent on engineered stormwater controls such as detention ponds, concrete culverts, and silt fencing.

- Air conditioning and utility bills can be reduced in well-landscaped commercial areas.

Shopping center with no landscaping

Shopping center with landscaping

Commercial district with no landscaping

Commercial district with landscaping

Landscaping, Charlottesville

Landscaping, Town of Elkton

FOR MORE INFORMATION:

Aesthetics of Parking: An Illustrated Guide, by Thomas P. Smith, PAS Report 411, 1988, American Planning Association; (312) 786-6344.

Preparing a Landscaping Ordinance, by Wendelyn A. Martz with Marya Morris, PAS Report 431, 1990, American Planning Association; (312) 786-6344.

Shading Our Cities: A Resource Guide for Urban and Community Forests, by American Forestry Association, Island Press, 1989; (202) 955-4500.

Trees Make Sense, by Elizabeth Brabec, Scenic America, Technical Information Series, Vol. I, No. I, 1992, Scenic America, Washington, DC; (202) 543-6200.

Value by Design: Landscaping, Site Planning and Amenities, Urban Land Institute, Washington, DC, 1994; (202) 624-7000.

Control Signs

Which street is more attractive? On which street are the signs easier to read?
Which street would you prefer to see in your community?

SIGN CONTROL is one of the most important and powerful actions a community can take to make an immediate visible improvement in its physical environment. This is because almost nothing will destroy the distinctive character of a community or region faster than uncontrolled signs and billboards. This doesn't mean we don't need signs. We do. Signs provide us with direction and needed information. As a planned, architectural feature a business sign can be colorful, decorative, even distinguished.

Willy nilly clutter and placement of signs can cause information overload and confusion.

Daniel Mandelker,
Street Graphics & The Law

A good sign code is pro-business, since an attractive business district will attract more customers than an ugly one. Moreover, when signs are controlled, businesses will do a better job of selling at less cost because when clutter is reduced, consumers actually have an easier time finding what they are looking for.

A community should consider guidelines for both public and private signs. The careful design and placement of traffic signs and all public signs can improve commu-

So why do Virginia communities need to control signs? The answer is obvious: too often signs are oversized, poorly planned, badly located, and altogether too numerous. What's more, sign clutter is ugly, costly, and ineffective. And it degrades one of Virginia's greatest economic assets—its scenic landscape.

Driving down a street cluttered with signs is often an unpleasant experience, not just because it is ugly but because it is fatiguing. Sign clutter overloads drivers with more information than is possible to manage. It requires great effort by the driver either to read it all or to block it all out, while attempting to drive safely.

Shopping center sign, Warrenton

nity appearance and aid drivers. A profusion of signs is as confusing as a lack of them.

Sign control is especially important to the health of Virginia's tourist-oriented economy. This is because the more the regions of our state come to look like every place else in America, the less reason there is to visit. On the other hand, the more Virginia communities do to enhance their unique assets—by protecting their visual character—the more people will want to visit.

THINGS YOU SHOULD KNOW:

■ A good sign communicates its message clearly and quickly, is compatible with its surroundings, and enhances the visual image of the community.

■ A good sign ordinance is clear and unambiguous, easy to understand, and easy to administer and enforce.

■ When the streetscape becomes overloaded with signs, the cumulative effect is negative. The viewer actually sees less, not more.

■ Many Virginia cities and counties prohibit billboards, among them Albemarle, Arlington, Botetourt, Clarke, Fairfax, Loudoun, James City, and Prince William counties.

■ There are no pole signs or billboards on the Capital Beltway around Washington, DC.

A good sign communicates simply and clearly.

A pole sign dominates the landscape.

A good sign is compatible with its surroundings.

Sign clutter is ugly, ineffective, and expensive.

This restaurant sign on Interstate 95 is the tallest sign in Virginia.

A much smaller sign for the same company in another community.

- Virginia's top tourist destinations—Williamsburg, Alexandria, and Virginia Beach—all have strong on-premise sign ordinances.

- Front Royal has used ISTEA Enhancements funds to remove non-conforming billboards. Contact: Front Royal's Director of Planning; (540) 635-4236.

FOR MORE INFORMATION:

"Sign Regulation, by Edward T. McMahon, *Planning Commissioners Journal,* Number 25, Winter 1996-1997; (802) 864-9083.

Sign Regulations for Small and Midsize Communities, by Eric Damien Kelly and Gary Raso, PAS Report 419, 1989, American Planning Association; (312) 786-6344.

Signs, Signs: A Video on the Economic and Environmental Benefits of Sign Control, Scenic America, Washington, DC; (202) 543-6200.

Street Graphics and the Law, by Daniel Mandelker and William Ewald, American Planning Association; (312) 786-6344.

Restrict Billboards

Which is a better, more effective, less environmentally harmful way to provide motorist information?

COME SEE AMERICA THE BEAUTIFUL, if you can. In some places, a drive in the country is more like a ride through the Yellow Pages—a windshield vista of 50-foot beer cans and towering gas station ads. Today hundreds of billboards line the major highways throughout Virginia, and in recent years Virginia billboards have gotten bigger, taller, and more intrusive than ever. What follows are eight reasons why Virginia communities should halt the proliferation of new billboards and work to reduce the number already in place.

1. Billboards are out of place in most locations.
Virginia's landscape is one of our greatest resources. Its value is economic as well as aesthetic; psychological as well as recreational. Each kind of landscape—farmland, mountains, forest, even urban—has its own kind of beauty, character, and uniqueness. In every kind of landscape, billboards are a disturbing, alien intrusion that mar scenic views, commercialize the countryside, and erode local community identity.

2. Billboards are a form of pollution—visual pollution. Regulating billboards is no different than regulating noxious fumes or sewage discharges. The U.S. Supreme Court has said, "Pollution is not limited to the air we breathe and the water we drink. It can equally offend the eye and ear." While the messages on billboards can be attractive, ugly, or just ordinary, when enlarged to 700 square feet, placed on poles 50-100 feet high, and randomly strewn along major highways, they become a form of litter—litter on a stick.

3. Billboards are the only form of advertisement you can't turn off or avoid. There is a vast difference between seeing an ad on a billboard versus seeing an ad, even the same one, in a magazine, newspaper, or on the television. When you buy a magazine or turn on the television, you exercise freedom of choice. You can easily close the magazine or shut off the television. In contrast, you have no power to turn off or throw away a billboard. Twenty-four hours a day, 365 days a year, billboards force advertising on individuals and communities whether they want to see it or not.

4. Billboard companies are selling something they don't own—our field of vision. Courts have long held that billboards do not derive their value from the private land they stand on, but from the public roads they stand next to. Courts call this the "parasite principle" because billboards feed like parasites off roads they pay nothing to build, use, or maintain. To understand this, imagine that every billboard in Virginia was turned around so that the message could not be seen from the road. They would suddenly be worthless. Their only value comes from being seen from public roadways.

5. **Billboard companies exercise almost no restraint in the placement of outdoor ads.**
Throughout America, billboard companies put billboards anywhere and everywhere they can. In urban areas, billboards can be found next to homes, schools, churches, parks, playgrounds, hospitals, even in cemeteries and historic districts. In the countryside, there is no area sufficiently rural or scenic to be safe from billboards. They're even found along many designated scenic byways!

6. **Billboards are both a cause and a symptom of community blight.** A cause, because billboards degrade the local environment, lower property values, and foster contempt for the public realm. A symptom, because one form of blight breeds another. Graffiti, trash, junk cars, billboards—where you find one, you'll often find the others.

7. **Billboard companies destroy trees on public land.** They do this to ensure that motorists see their signs instead of our scenery. The billboard industry calls this practice "vegetation management," but it is actually the destruction of public property for private gain. In addition to chain-sawing trees, billboard companies often spray herbicides to kill existing plants and to guarantee that nothing grows in their place. The destruction of trees and the use of herbicides contribute to groundwater pollution, soil erosion, and wildlife habitat destruction.

8. **Billboards are ineffective and unnecessary.**
There are alternatives to billboards that provide the same information at less cost without degrading our landscape. What's more, billboards are one of the least effective forms of advertising. Most billboards simply advertize products or services which have nothing to do with motorist information—beer, shoes, TV shows, etc. They are a secondary form of advertising that is used to reinforce ads in other media. Consumer spending is not any lower in those communities—such as Arlington, Alexandria, Williamsburg, Fairfax County or Loudoun County—where billboards are prohibited. On the contrary, the cities and states that totally ban billboards—such as Alaska, Hawaii, Maine, and Vermont—are among America's leading tourist destinations.

FOR MORE INFORMATION:

Fighting Billboard Blight: An Action Guide for Citizens and Public Officials, by Frank Vespe, Scenic America, 1999; (202) 543-6200.

Visual Pollution and Sign Control: A Legal Handbook, by Kay Slaughter, Southern Environmental Law Center; (804) 977-4090.

Tree cut in front of a billboard

Disguise Communication Towers

Did you know that cell towers can be disguised as flagpoles, silos, church steeples, or even trees?

THE COMMUNICATIONS REVOLUTION means that cellular telephone towers are proliferating. In some parts of the country, communication towers now loom above every hillside and more are coming. Fortunately, there are a number of legal and politically acceptable alternatives to cell tower proliferation. Wireless communication companies can share cell sites, and cell sites can be hidden, disguised, or otherwise made less obtrusive. See the examples on the next page.

THINGS YOU SHOULD KNOW:

- Thousands of cellular telephone towers will be built in Virginia in the coming decade. Just 15 years ago, mobile phones were a novelty item. But by 1990, 10 million people were using cellular phones and over the past decade, the number of cell phone subscribers has skyrocketed to more than 70 million.

- *The Wall Street Journal* reports that 22,000 cellular communications sites have been built in the U.S. over the past 15 years, and they predict that another 100,000 will be built in the coming years.

- Sites on ridge lines and mountaintops offer maximum "coverage." In fact, many of the most efficient locations for cell phone towers are unfortunately the most visually conspicuous. In these locations, towers can be hundreds of feet tall.

- In 1996, Congress passed the Federal Telecommunications Act, portions of which prevent municipalities from banning cellular phone towers outright, assuring that the industry will eventually be able to provide a maximum standard of mobile phone coverage in most places. But the 1996 Act also allows municipalities to regulate cell tower construction through local laws in order to minimize visual and other impacts.

- Since wireless communications technology is so new and has grown so fast, many local governments are not adequately prepared to regulate tower siting and construction.

- The courts have ruled that wireless communications companies should be classified as "public utilities," and that as such they are entitled to preferential treatment with regard to zoning regulations and the issuance of use variances.

- Forward-thinking communities need to adopt a separate test for use variances that would apply specifically to any public utility proposing to build a cell tower. Possible tests might, for example, include the need for companies to prove that the tower is truly needed to meet their required standards for service, and that no alternative sites are suitable for that purpose or that no other existing towers can be used.

■ A local law that allows the presence of towers by special temporary use permit is a good first step. The temporary special use permit can be renewable every five years. This can help ensure that towers will be removed if they are abandoned or become obsolete.

■ Local governments also are permitted to adopt land-use regulations that require towers to meet aesthetic standards through the special permit or the site plan approval process. The most standard technique is to require that towers be disguised as flagpoles, silos, or even trees. Or they can be required to be placed on existing structures such as water towers, electricity transmission towers, tall buildings, even inside church steeples. Municipal regulations can require the co-location of transmitters on existing towers, whenever feasible. Co-location precludes the need for additional towers.

Cell tower on electric lines

Combined cell/water tower

Cell tower disguised as tree

FOR MORE INFORMATION:

Implementing the New Telecommunications Law, American Planning Association, 1996. This 33-page guidebook is part of an information packet on cellular communication towers prepared by APA's Planning Advisory Service; (312) 786-6344.

Siting Cellular Towers, by the National League of Cities, available from American Planning Association; (312) 786-6344.

"Wireless Communication Facilities Issues Paper," San Diego Association of Governments, 1995. Obtainable by sending a check for $5.00 to SANDAG, 401 B Street, Suite 800, San Diego, CA 92101; (619) 595-5300.

Design Streets for Healthy Neighborhoods

Which street is better for the environment? Safer for children? More affordable to construct?

Overly wide neighborhood streets encourage speeding, generate stormwater run-off and non-point-source pollution, and increase the cost of new houses along the street. Traditional streets, on the other hand, provide for healthy neighborhoods and livable communities. Traditional streets, which were the norm before World War II, are designed for use by people, not just motor vehicles. Such streets are designed for low speed (15-20 mph) and typically provide sidewalks, on-street parking, shade trees, and other community amenities.

These design elements combine to create an environment that encourages walking, bicycling, and a sense of community. Traditional streets are narrower than conventional streets, and they are well connected to distribute motor vehicle traffic and to provide a variety of places to walk. Traditional streets have blocks no longer than 300-450 feet, and intersections have turning radii that require low speeds, yet allow access by

> *Our most valued places are often sites which lack our most valued possession: cars.*
>
> David Sucher, *City of Comforts*

emergency and service vehicles. Traditional streets are safer for children because traffic volume and speed are reduced. Traditional streets are also better for the environment because less pavement means less run-off, less soil erosion, and less non-point-source pollution. Traditional streets are also less expensive to construct and provide developers and realtors with a marketing advantage over subdivisions with conventional streets.

THINGS YOU SHOULD KNOW:

- The conventional approach to street design aims to move more traffic faster at the expense of everything else. However, accommodating cars and trucks is only one of a street's functions.

- Since there are so few destinations or amenities within conventional subdivisions, residents must typically make 10 to 12 car trips per household per day. Children must be driven or take the bus to school and parents must spend the weekend chauffeuring their children everywhere.

- Conventional street design encourages motorists to speed through neighborhoods at 35 or even 45 mph. Typically, the wider the street, the faster the cars go.

- When pedestrians are hit by cars going 40 to 45 mph, they die 83 percent of the time. On the other hand, if a pedestrian is hit by a car going 20 mph or less, the fatality rate falls to 3-5 percent.

- Traditional streets are really like outdoor rooms; cars are slowed and pedestrian comfort is increased by adding street trees, on-street parking, sidewalks and placing buildings closer to the street.

- Traditional neighborhoods often have neighborhood schools, parks, churches, small stores and other attractions to which people can walk.

This private lane in Loudoun County is narrower than a typical subdivision street.

- Before Walt Disney Corporation built Celebration, its new traditional town in Florida, it conducted an extensive market study of what homebuyers wanted. Their study found that 50 percent of Americans wanted to live in a village-style community or a traditional neighborhood.

- However, since only one percent of new development is designed to replicate older traditional patterns, a major demand for neighborhoods that retain small-town living styles goes unfulfilled.

FOR MORE INFORMATION:

Residential Streets, 2nd edition, American Society of Civil Engineers, National Association of Homebuilders and Urban Land Institute, 1990; (202) 624-7000.

Street Design Guidelines for Healthy Neighborhoods, by Dan Burden, Center for Livable Communities, 1999; (800) 290-8202.

Take Back Your Streets: How to Protect Communities from Asphalt and Traffic, Conservation Law Foundation, 1998; (617) 350-0990.

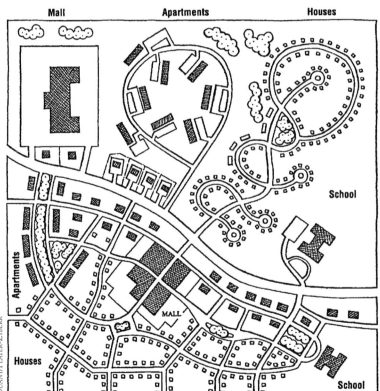

Top: Conventional development with poor connectivity causes congestion and discourages pedestrians and cyclists. Bottom: Better development with interconnected street system allows more transportation options and shorter trips.

Build Trails and Greenways

Would you rather live in a community where you have to drive everywhere for everything, or in a community where you can walk, ride a bicycle, or drive to where you want to go?

WALKING FOR PLEASURE is the single most popular form of outdoor recreation in America today. Yet, in many Virginia communities, there are few places to walk, except on neighborhood streets. As a result, the popularity of bicycle and pedestrian facilities has risen tremendously in recent years. In 1992, the Virginia Outdoors Survey found that 48% of Virginians ranked the provision of additional hiking and walking trails as the state's most important outdoor recreation resource need. An additional 42% think bicycle trails are the state's top recreation resource need. Many Virginia communities are finding that walking trails, bike paths, and greenways are popular, safe, and cost-effective ways to provide

more opportunities for hiking, walking, bicycling, jogging, roller-blading, and other popular outdoor activities. Here are some examples:

THINGS YOU SHOULD KNOW:

■ Walking and bicycling improve personal health and fitness.

■ Walking and bicycling for transportation remove cars from the roads and ease traffic congestion.

■ Bicycling means there are fewer cars emitting pollution, which improves air quality. It also saves money since less is spent on car maintenance and gasoline.

■ Walking and bicycling create a sense of community by promoting social interaction with neighbors, co-workers, and other local citizens.

■ Many studies demonstrate that walking trails and bicycle paths increase nearby property values. In turn, increased property values can increase local tax revenues.

■ Spending by local residents on trail-related activities helps support recreation-oriented businesses and

W & OD Trail, Herndon

employment, like bicycle shops and sporting goods stores.

- Greenways often provide new business opportunities and locations for commercial activities such as bed and breakfasts, recreation equipment rentals and sales, and other related businesses.

- Evidence shows that the quality of life of a community is an increasingly important factor in corporate relocation decisions. Trails and greenways are often cited as important contributors to quality of life.

EXAMPLES FROM ACROSS THE STATE:

- Virginia's New River Trail State Park is a major tourist attraction that generates expenditures on lodging, food, and recreation-oriented services.

- The Washington and Old Dominion (W&OD) Trail in Northern Virginia is the nation's most popular rail-trail, used by almost 2 million people each year. The Regional Park Authority managing the trail gets $450,000 a year from fiber-optic license fees, rental fees, and other sources.

- The Town of Blacksburg adopted a Bikeway/Walkway Master Plan as part of its comprehensive plan. Pedestrian access to adjoining parcels is required.

- A developer who donated a 50-foot-wide, 7-mile-long easement along a trail near Front Royal sold all 50 parcels bordering the trail in only two months.

- The Sherando Area Bicycle and Pedestrian Facility will link high-density residential and commercial areas in Frederick County with a regional park and a high school. An ISTEA grant is funding the 2.45-mile first phase.

- Waynesboro is planning a greenway to link the city's parks and provide a trail along the South River, a dominant feature that runs through the City.

Riverwalk, Alexandria

Path near Arboretum, Harrisonburg

© ROCKINGHAM COUNTY PLANNING DEPT.

Blackwater Creek Trail, Lynchburg

C&O Canal towpath, Potomac, Md.

Bike lane, Charlottesville

- Rivanna Trails Foundation, a volunteer organization in Albemarle County, is working to create a greenbelt around Charlottesville.

FOR MORE INFORMATION:

The Economic Benefits of Parks and Open Space, by Steve Lerner and William Poole, Trust for Public Land, 1999; (415) 495-4103.

Economic Impacts of Protecting Rivers, Trails, and Greenway Corridors, by the National Park Service's Rivers and Trails Conservation Assistance Program, 1994. Available through the Trails and Greenways Clearinghouse; (877) GRNWAYS.

Greenways: A Guide to Planning, Design, and Development, by Chuck Flink, Loring Schwartz, and Robert Searns, Island Press, 1995. Available through The Conservation Fund; (703) 525-6300.

Thinking Green, A Guide to the Benefits and Costs of Greenways and Trails, Florida Department of Environmental Protection, 1998. Available from Office of Greenways and Trails, 2600 Blairstone Road, MS 795, Tallahassee, FL 32399; (850) 488-3701.

Virginia Trails Association, P.O. Box 1232, Ashland, VA 23005; (804) 798-4160.

Reassess Road Standards

Shouldn't new highways protect neighborhoods and quality of life in the communities they traverse?

EACH YEAR VIRGINIA COMMUNITIES are presented with plans to expand streets and roads. Whether the community is urban or rural, in Northern Virginia or on the Eastern Shore, the explanation is almost always the same. A road that local people are accustomed to is said to be deficient. It does not conform to the latest standards. It is not wide enough or it has too many curves. Unless something is done, motorists will experience delays that highway engineers consider excessive.

Plans are presented that call for a road that is straighter, flatter, and above all wider than before. The highway department calls the project a road "improvement," but many local people are opposed to the project. Why? Because conventional road widening projects often damage scenery, historic integrity, livability and community character for little or no real benefit.

The conventional approach to road design aims to move more traffic faster at the expense of everything else. In her book *The Living City*, author Roberta Gratz tells the story of a small town that seeks help with repairs to an aging bridge, only to be told that repairing the bridge is "not cost efficient." Only by widening the two lane bridge to four lanes would federal funds be available. Adding two lanes, however, will require

widening and straightening the road that provides access to the bridge. This will require condemning adjacent park land, cutting down a row of 100-year-old trees, and demolishing several historic buildings. When local residents oppose the out-of-scale solution, they are accused of opposing progress and they are told federal rules "require" the new wider bridge.

Does this sound familiar? Well, it should because this scenario, in one form or another, is being repeated throughout America. Overscaled, overpriced highway projects are imposed where smaller, less expensive, equally useful, and more environmentally benign solutions would do.

Citizens protest road widening, Warren County

While ugly, overscaled highway projects are familiar to us all, the good news is that the Virginia Department of Transportation (VDOT) is becoming more sensitive to community needs, and new federal transportation legislation now gives states the flexibility to use their own design standards in sensitive locations. What's more, federal law also makes it clear that highway projects should be designed with social, environmental, and cultural resources in mind.

THINGS YOU SHOULD KNOW:

- Many transportation experts say the key to eliminating traffic congestion is planning transportation systems in concert with land uses.

- *A Policy on Geometric Design of Streets and Highways,* also known as the AASHTO Green Book, is a publication that sets out recommended design standards for all federal aid highway projects.

- Controversy over design standards often arises when state DOTs take the Green Book standards and apply them in a rigid and unyielding fashion without regard for community or environmental impacts.

Attractive bridge railings like this will be replaced with Jersey barriers, unless Virginia communities request more sensitive designs.

- Federal law says these standards "can be applied flexibly," and the Federal Highway Administration (FHWA) has produced an easy-to-read manual that thoroughly discusses the issues of design flexibility in federally funded highway or road projects. This publication, *Flexibility in Highway Design,* can be obtained from the FHWA (for ordering details, see the "For more information" section).

- Whereas the Green Book was based on the assumption that standards should meet the needs of motor vehicles, newer legislation, particularly the Intermodal Surface Transportation Efficiency Act of 1991 (ISTEA) and the Transportation Equity Act of 1998 (TEA-21), recognize the importance of pedestrians as well as social, environmental and visual resources.

- For example, reducing the speed limit on a road through an historic village can be just as effective in reducing accidents as widening the shoulder by ten feet.

- Vermont has developed road design standards that are more flexible than AASHTO's. The standards stress the importance of considering a road's context and setting in all design decisions so that highway facilities complement Vermont's built and natural environment.

- Five other states—Connecticut, Kentucky, Maryland, Minnesota, and Utah—are working on a FHWA-sponsored pilot project to develop context-sensitive highway design standards.

- The Route 50 Corridor Coalition in the Virginia Piedmont has developed a "traffic calming" plan for U.S. 50 as an alternative to the road widening and bypass plans originally proposed by VDOT. The traffic calming plan was approved for $13 million in federal funding, and its implementation is underway.

- Confronted with VDOT's plan to "improve" a portion of the Snickersville Turnpike, a Virginia Byway running from Aldie to Bluemont, citizens organized to develop their own, much less intrusive, plan for the road corridor. Eventually VDOT compromised on the width of the improved road and shoulders, and it used material that was more considerate of the road's scenic and historic character.

- In the United States, roads and asphalt parking lots cover more than 38 million acres.

- A road commission has recommended widening all 325 miles of Interstate 81 to six or eight lanes. The project would cost over $3.5 billion and take 15-20 years to complete.

Blue Ridge Parkway, Virginia

- The proposed 12-lane bridge across the Potomac River near Old Town Alexandria would cost more than $2 billion.

Reduce the Impact of the Car

FOR MORE INFORMATION:

Aesthetic Guidelines for Bridge Design, Minnesota Department of Transportation, 1995. Available for $32.50 from MNDOT, (651) 582-1104.

Flexibility in Highway Design, Federal Highway Administration, FHWA-PD-97-062, 1997. Available free from the Scenic Byways Clearinghouse, (800) BYWAYS.

A State Highway Project in Your Town? Your Role and Rights: A Primer for Citizens and Public Officials, by Jim Wick, Preservation Trust of Vermont, 1995. Available for $13 from the Preservation Trust of Vermont, 104 Church Street, Burlington, VT 05401; (802) 658-6647.

A Traffic Calming Plan for Virginia's Rural Route 50 Corridor, Route 50 Corridor Coalition, Middleburg, Virginia, 1996. Available from the Route 50 Corridor Coalition, (540) 687-4055.

Traffic Calming: The Solution to Urban Traffic and a New Vision for Neighborhood Livability, available from Citizens for Sensible Transportation, (503) 225-0003.

Designate Scenic Byways

Would you prefer a scenic drive with views like this—or this?

SCENIC BYWAYS are "the roads less traveled"—roads that provide leisurely driving through areas rich in history and natural beauty. Driving for pleasure is the second most popular recreational activity in America (after walking), and scenic byways are the avenues that foster that activity. They open up vistas and introduce us to places we might otherwise pass by.

Scenic byways promote tourism and resource protection simultaneously. They are a framework for regional planning and a way to link communities along a byway corridor to enhance community well-being.

In 1991, ISTEA established the National Scenic Byways Program for the designation of National Scenic Byways and All American Roads (the best of the best). Nominations come from grassroots communities through the states to the Federal Highway Administration. Each road nominated must have a corridor management plan prepared through local citizens participation and consensus. As of 1999, nine All American Roads and 53 National Scenic Byways had been designated nationwide.

Most states have scenic byways programs as well. The Virginia Byway program was created in the early 1960s, and by 1999, some 200 Virginia Byway segments had been designated, approximately 1,700 miles. Virginia Byways can be found in 52 counties and two cities—Richmond and Williamsburg. Only one part of the state is lacking in designations: the Tidewater region north of the York River has no Virginia Byways.

Although a federal highway regulation prohibits new billboards on scenic byways, byway designation in Virginia does little to protect road corridors against highway widening, tree removal, or unsightly roadside development. The Virginia DOT needs to do more to strengthen the Virginia Byway program so that it protects, as well as promotes, special road corridors.

THINGS YOU SHOULD KNOW:

- According to a study by the U.S. Travel Data Center, travelers spent almost $48 million annually while traveling on 1,600 miles of designated National Scenic Byways around the country.

- "Lee's Retreat" provides a popular tourist driving experience from Petersburg to Appomattox that traces Lee's route in the final days of the Confederacy. Along the route, interpretive kiosks tell the story of Lee's Army and of the Virginia landscape.

■ A Concept Plan has been developed for the Staunton-to-Parkersburg Pike by the Valley Conservation Council. The plan lays out a vision for the corridor and presents a discussion of strategies for protecting and interpreting the multiple historic, scenic, agricultural, and natural features of the region through which it passes.

■ Route 15 from Gettysburg, Pa., to Charlottesville has been named "Journey Through Hallowed Ground" because of its importance in linking key Civil War battlegrounds and sites. National and regional organizations are working to ensure that Route 15 remains a viable scenic and historic transportation corridor.

■ Through a two-year effort, a corridor management plan has been prepared for Route 13 on the Eastern Shore. The plan articulates a vision for this 68-mile-long corridor to ensure its long-term role in enhancing the region's economy and conserving natural and cultural resources.

Colonial Parkway

■ "Drive Through History" is a self-guided auto tour through the John S. Mosby Heritage Area in Virginia's Piedmont. This tour along historic Route 50 from Aldie to Paris at the foot of the Blue Ridge is an immensely popular heritage tourism route.

■ A survey of Blue Ridge Parkway users showed that in 1995 nonresident Parkway visitors spent about $264 per trip in Virginia counties along the parkway. This amounts to more than $904 million in direct and indirect expenditures per year.

Reduce the Impact of the Car

FOR MORE INFORMATION:

Community Guide to Planning & Managing a Scenic Byway, U.S. Department of Transportation, Federal Highway Administration. To order, call the National Scenic Byways Resource Center, (800) 429-9297.

Design Guide for Rural Roads, Dutchess Land Conservancy, 1998, (914) 677-3002.

The McDowell Battlefield Staunton-to-Parkersburg Pike Concept Plan (1996) and *McDowell Battlefield Landowners Guide* (1999), Valley Conservation Council; (540) 886-3541.

Saving Historic Roads, by Paul Daniel Marriott, New York: John Wiley & Sons, 1998, (800) 225-5945.

Appendix: ORGANIZATIONAL RESOURCES

VIRGINIA STATE AGENCIES

Virginia Department of Conservation and Recreation
203 Governor Street, Suite 302
Richmond, VA 23219
(804) 786-6124
www.dcr.state.va.us

Virginia Department of Forestry
Fontaine Research Park
900 Natural Resources Drive, Suite 800
Charlottesville, Virginia 22903
(804) 977-6555
www.dof.state.va.us

Virginia Department of Historic Resources
2801 Kensington Avenue
Richmond, VA 23221
(804) 367-2323
www.dhr.state.va.us

Virginia Department of Transportation
1401 East Broad Street
Richmond, VA 23219
(804) 371-6752 (Environmental Programs)
(804) 786-2264 (Enhancements)
www.vdot.state.va.us

Virginia Main Street Program
Virginia Department of Housing and Community Development
501 N. Second Street
Richmond, VA 23219
(804) 371-7030
www.dhcd.state.va.us

Virginia Outdoors Foundation
Richmond Office
203 Governor Street, Suite 316
Richmond, VA 23219
(804) 225-2147 (Richmond office)
(703) 327-6118 (Northern Virginia office)
(804) 293-3423 (Charlottesville office)
(540) 886-2460 (Shenandoah Valley office)
(540) 951-2822 (Western Virginia office)

VIRGINIA ORGANIZATIONS

Central Virginia Battlefields Trust
604-A William Street, Suite 1
Fredericksburg, VA 22401
(540) 371-4157
www.cvbt.org
The Central Virginia Battlefields Trust works to purchase and preserve significant Civil War battlefields and landmarks. It also serves as an advocate for battlefield preservation.

Chesapeake Bay Foundation
1008 E. Main Street, Suite 1600
Richmond, VA 23219
(804) 780-1392
www.cbf.org
The Chesapeake Bay Foundation acts to restore and sustain the bay's ecosystem by improving water clarity, diversity, and abundance of living resources in the watershed.

James River Association

P.O. Box 110
Richmond, VA 23218-0110
(804) 730-2898
www.jamesriverassociation.org
The James River Association works to encourage sustainable growth in the James River Watershed that is consistent with the conservation of natural and historic resources.

Land Trust of Virginia

P.O. Box 354
Leesburg, VA 20178
(540) 687-8441
The Land Trust of Virginia works with local communities, primarily through conservation easements, to meet their historical and natural resource objectives.

New Dominion Business Council

P.O. Box 1124
Leesburg, VA 20177
(703) 771-3301
The New Dominion Business Council was formed to provide the business community with a forum for advocating for responsible growth.

Northern Virginia Conservation Trust

4022 Hummer Road
Annandale, VA 22003
(703) 354-5093Ã
The Northern Virginia Conservation Trust works to preserve open space in Arlington, Fairfax, Prince William, and other Northern Virginia counties.

Piedmont Environmental Council

P.O. Box 460
Warrenton, VA 20188
(540) 347-2334
www.pec-va.org
The Piedmont Environmental Council works to preserve the rural economy, natural resources, history, and beauty of the Northern Piedmont region of Virginia. PEC also provides technical assistance on land use policy and land conservation.

Potomac Conservancy

4022 Hummer Road
Annandale, VA 22003
(703) 642-9880
The Potomac Conservancy works to preserve the natural, historic and recreational qualities of the Potomac River.

Preservation Alliance of Virginia

700 Harris Street, Suite 106
Charlottesville, VA 22902
(804) 421-9800
www.vapreservation.org
The Preservation Alliance works to preserve and promote the cultural, historic, architectural and archaeological heritage of the Commonwealth.

Scenic Virginia

P.O. Box 17606
Richmond, VA 23226
(804) 282-5522
www.scenicva.org
Scenic Virginia, Inc., works to protect, preserve and enhance the scenic beauty of the Commonwealth of Virginia. It provides information on highway beautification, scenic byway designation, and sign control.

Shenandoah Valley Battlefields
National Historic District Commission

P.O. Box 897
New Market, VA 22844
(540) 740-4543
www.valleybattlefields.org
The commission was created by federal legislation in November 1996 to develop a management plan to protect the resources of the Shenandoah Valley Battlefields National Historic District.

Southern Environmental Law Center
201 W. Main Street, Suite 14
Charlottesville, VA 22902
(804) 977-4090
www.southernenvironment.org
SELC is the only environmental organization dedicated solely to protecting the natural resources of the southeastern United States.

Valley Conservation Council
P.O. Box 2335
Staunton, VA 24402
(540) 886-3541
www.valleyconservation.org
The Valley Conservation Council works to promote land uses that sustain the farms, forests, open spaces and cultural heritage of the Valley region of Virginia.

Virginia Conservation Network
1001 E. Broad Street, Suite 410
Richmond, VA 23219
(804) 644-0283
www.vcnva.org
The Virginia Conservation Network (VCN) is a coalition of organizations devoted to advancing a common, environmentally sound vision for Virginia.

Virginia Trails Association
P.O. Box 1132
Ashland, VA 23005
(804) 798-4160
The Virginia Trails Association promotes the development of trails and greenways throughout Virginia.

Western Virginia Land Trust
P.O. Box 18102
Roanoke, VA 24101-0000
(540) 985-0000
The Western Virginia Land Trust works to protect open space, natural areas and scenic landscapes in southwestern Virginia.

Williamsburg Land Conservancy
5000 New Point Road, Suite 1202
Williamsburg, VA 23188
(757) 565-0343
www.wmbglandconserv.org
The Williamsburg Land Conservancy works to preserve historic, scenic and environmentally sensitive lands in the James and York River Basins.

NATIONAL ORGANIZATIONS

American Farmland Trust
1200 18th Street, N.W., Suite 800
Washington, DC 20036
(202) 331-7300
www.farmland.org
The leading conservation organization dedicated to protecting America's agricultural resources. AFT provides a variety of information resources and services.

American Forests
910 17th Street, N.W., Suite 600
Washington, DC 20006
(202) 955-4500
www.amfor.org
The oldest citizen's conservation organization in the U.S., American Forests provides information on urban forestry, tree preservation, and reforestation.

American Planning Association
122 S. Michigan Ave., Suite 1600
Chicago, IL 60603
(312) 431-9100 (general)
(312) 786-6344 (Planning Advisory service and Planners Book Service)
www.planning.org
The American Planning Association provides informational services, education, and research on all aspects of city and regional planning.

Civil War Preservation Trust

1515 Wilson Boulevard, Suite 350

Arlington, VA 22209

(703) 682-2350

www.civilwar.org

The mission of The Civil War Trust is to preserve significant Civil War battlefields and to support preservation education programs.

Coalition for Smarter Growth

1415 Oronoco Street

Alexandria, VA 22314

(703) 683-5704

stopsprawl@aol.com

The Coalition for Smart Growth advocates better land use and transit-oriented design in Northern Virginia.

Congress for the New Urbanism

5 Third Street, Suite 725

San Francisco, CA 94103

(415) 495-2255

www.cnu.org

The Congress for the New Urbanism advocates restructuring public policy and development practices to support the restoration of existing urban centers and towns within coherent metropolitan regions.

The Conservation Fund

1800 North Kent Street, Suite 1120

Arlington, VA 22209-2156

(703) 525-6300

www.conservationfund.org

The Conservation Fund works to protect open space, wildlife habitat, and historic sites throughout America. The Fund also assists business, government, and the nonprofit sector with projects that integrate economic development with environmental protection.

Joint Center for Sustainable Communities

c/o U.S. Conference of Mayors

1620 Eye Street, N.W.

Washington, DC 20006

(202) 293-7330

www.usmayors.org/USCM/sustainble

The Joint Center for Sustainable Communities provides a forum for cities and counties to work together to develop long-term policies and programs that will lead to job growth, environmental stewardship and social equity.

Land Trust Alliance

1331 H St., N.W., Suite 400

Washington, DC 20005-4711

(202) 638-4725

www.lta.org

The Land Trust Alliance provides services and programs for local and regional land trusts. It also provides information on all aspects of private land conservation, including easements and fee acquisition.

National Arbor Day Foundation

211 N. 12th Street, Suite 501

Lincoln, NE 68508

(402) 474-5655

www.arborday.org

The National Arbor Day Foundation sponsors programs and publishes information encouraging the conservation of trees.

National Main Street Center

c/o National Trust for Historic Preservation

1785 Massachusetts Avenue, N.W.

Washington, DC 20036

(202) 588-6219

www.mainst.org

The National Main Street Center works with communities across the nation to revitalize their traditional downtowns and neighborhood commercial areas. It provides information on downtown revitalization.

National Scenic Byways Resource Center

227 West First Street, Suite 610

Duluth, MN 55802

(800) 429-9297

www.byways.org

Sponsored by the Federal Highway Administration (FHWA), it provides information on all aspects of scenic byways.

National Trust for Historic Preservation

1785 Massachusetts Ave., N.W.

Washington, DC 20036

(202) 588-6000

www.nthp.org

The National Trust for Historic Preservation works to protect the irreplaceable. It fights to save historic buildings, neighborhoods, and landscapes. It provides information on all aspects of historic preservation.

The Nature Conservancy

4245 N. Fairfax Drive, Suite 100

Arlington, VA 22203

(703) 841-5300

www.tnc.org

The Nature Conservancy works to preserve plants, animals and natural communities that represent the diversity of life on Earth by protecting lands and waters they need to survive.

Scenic America

801 Pennsylvania Ave., S.E., Suite 300

Washington, DC 20003-2152

(202) 543-6200

www.scenic.org

Scenic America works to preserve and enhance the scenic character of America's communities and countryside. It provides information on sign control, tree preservation and other forms of landscape protection.

Sprawl Watch Clearinghouse

1100 17th Street, N.W., 10th Floor

Washington, DC 20036

(202) 332-7000

www.sprawlwatch.org

The Sprawl Watch Clearinghouse makes the tools, techniques, and strategies for managing growth accessible to citizens, grassroots organizations, environmentalists, public officials, planners, architects, the media and business leaders.

Surface Transportation Policy Project

1100 17th Street, N.W., 10th Floor

Washington, DC 20036

(202) 466-2636

www.transact.org/stpp.htm

The Surface Transportation Policy Project works to ensure that transportation policy and investments help conserve energy, protect environmental and aesthetic quality, strengthen the economy, promote social equity, and make communities more livable.

Trails and Greenways Clearinghouse

1100 17th Street, N.W., 10th Floor

Washington, DC 20036

(877) GRN.W.AYS (toll-free)

www.trailsandgreenways.org

The Trails and Greenways Clearinghouse provides technical assistance, information resources and referrals to trail and greenway advocates and developers across the nation.

Trust for Public Land

116 New Montgomery Street, 4th Floor

San Francisco, CA 94105

(415) 495-4014

www.tpl.org

The Trust for Public Land conserves land for people to improve the quality of life for our communities.

Urban Land Institute

1025 Thomas Jefferson St., N.W., Suite 500 West

Washington, DC 20007

(202) 624-7000

www.uli.org

The Urban Land Institute provides leadership in the responsible use of land to enhance the total environment. ULI offers a wide variety of books and materials on development issues.

Useful Websites

Organization/Agency/Community	Web Address	Telephone
American Farmland Trust	www.farmland.org	202-331-7300
American Institute of Architects	www.e-architect.com	800-290-8202
American Planning Association	www.planning.org	312-431-9100
Chesapeake Bay Foundation	www.savethebay.cbf.org	804-780-1392
Congress for the New Urbanism	www.cnu.org	415-495-2255
The Conservation Fund	www.conservationfund.org	703-525-6300
U.S. Environmental Protection Agency	www.epa.gov	202-260-2090
International City/County Management Assn.	www.icma.org	202-289-4262
Land Trust Alliance	www.lta.org	202-638-4725
National Association of Homebuilders	www.nahb.com	800-368-5242
National League of Cities	www.nlc.org	202-626-3000
National Trust for Historic Preservation	www.nthp.org	202-588-6000
Piedmont Environmental Council	www.pec-va.org	540-347-2334
Planning Commissioners Journal	www.plannersweb.com	802-864-9083
Preservation Alliance of Virginia	www.vapreservation.org	804-421-9800
Scenic Virginia	www.scenicva.org	804-282-5522
Smart Growth Network	www.smartgrowth.org	202-260-2750
Southern Environmental Law Center	www.southernenvironment.org	804-977-4090
Sprawl Watch Clearinghouse	www.sprawlwatch.org	202-332-7000
State of Maryland—Smart Growth and Neighborhood Conservation	www.op.state.md.us/ smartgrowth/index.html	410-260-8112
Surface Transportation Policy Project	www.transact.org	202-466-2636
Sustainable Communities Network	www.sustainable.org	
The Trust for Public Land	www.tpl.org	415-495-4014
U.S. Conference of Mayors—Joint Center for Sustainable Communities	www.usmayors.org/USCM/ sustainable	202-861-6784 or 202-942-4224
Urban Land Institute	www.uli.org	202-661-8805
Valley Conservation Council	www.valleyconservation.org	540-886-3541
Virginia Center for Stewardship	www.sustainableusa.org/va	703-750-6401
Virginia Conservation Network	www.vcnva.org	804- 644- 0283
Trails and Greenways Clearinghouse	www.trailsandgreenways.org	877- GRNWAYS